COSMIC BIBLE

Paradigm Revolution
by Paradoxical Truth

BOOK 3

Minoru Uba

Copyright © 2015 by Minoru Uba

COSMIC BIBLE BOOK 3

Published by Babel Press U.S.A.
All rights reserved.
Date of publication: July 4, 2015

This book was originally published in Japanese under the title "宇宙聖書" by VOICE, Japan in 2010.

Author: Minoru Uba

Director: Tomoki Hotta

Original translation by Self-Healing Study and Practice Group
Edited and translated by Gyoko Koike

Coordinator: Junko Rodriguez
Formatting: Sota Torigoe

ISBN: 978-0989232647

Babel Corporation
Pacific Business News Bldg. #208,
1833 Kalakaua Avenue,
Honolulu, Hawaii 96815

Phone: (808) 946 - 3773
Fax: (808) 946 - 3993

Website: http://www.bookandright.com/

CONTENTS

Chapter Three☆The Turning Point

3-1. Limit of the finite theory of the universe…..11
3-2. Universe is the perfect collaboration…..11
3-3. "Relative universal original power" and proof of relativity of the universe…..13
3-4. SHINSEI (true sense) and the "rule of original creation power" in the universe…..18
3-5. SHINSEI is not the only and absolute existence…..21
3-6. The views of God dispelled by the PARAREVO theory…..24
3-7. Mechanisms of infinity of the universe…..25
3-8. Imperfection of the relative fluctuation is the driving force for evolution…..26
3-9. The "rule of preservation by inscription" based on "All worldly things are impermanent"…..30
3-10. Physical world benefits and spiritual world benefits are the opposite sides of the coin…..33
3-11. Energy waves in material world and spiritual world…..35
3-12. Memory is always trying to preserve higher inscription…..36
3-13. The complex three-dimensional structure of SHINSEI, the soul, and the body…..37
3-14. The definition and the rules of SHINSEI…..38
3-15. Spiritual world benefits and physical world benefits based on the principle of freedom…..39
3-16. The "rule of reincarnation" is the curse and bind of instinctive survival consciousnesses…..41
3-17. The "rule of relative conversion" in the qualitative world and the quantitative world…..44
3-18. The "rule of reincarnation" of the quantitative world in the earth star…..46

3-19. The qualitative world and quantitative world are reverse vector…..48
3-20. The importance of verifying the spiritual dimension…..52
3-21. The universe directs to dimensional integration…..53
3-22. The PARAREVO theory and the equations for spiritual evolution…..54
3-23. The criterion of love in the sentiment world determines the 10 levels of spiritual dimensions…..55
3-24. Gradual stages of the sentiment world in the spiritual dimension…..58
3-25. The criterion of mind and spirit determines the 10 levels of spiritual consciousness entities…..60
3-26. The 10 levels of the criterion of physical desire…..62
3-27. The criterion of spirit and mind of the 6 stages in the level of the earth…..64
3-28. The equation for "regeneration of SHINSEI and soul"…..67
3-29. The relative original power with trinity of Sun, Moon, and Earth…..68
3-30. Substantial relative original power with the moon…..70
3-31. The energy wave of the moon and atomic conversion…..71
3-32. The difference of physical effects between the new moon and the full moon…..72
3-33. Possible methods to make energy conversion of water molecules…..73
3-34. Dependency on water and the principle of domination…..76
3-35. The world of SHINSEI integration consciousness is infinite …..77
3-36. The release of the body from oxygen domination…..78
3-37. Hydrogen was the first element in the universe…..80
3-38. Excessive oxygen domination makes active oxygen…..81
3-39. Ancient lives succeeded in obtaining oxygen…..83
3-40. Mechanism of respiration and oxidation…..84

3-41. The energy wave of the moon is the border between the spiritual world and this world…..86
3-42. Roles and responsibilities of the moon toward the earth…..88
3-43. Solar energy waves affect the mind…..91
3-44. Solar energy waves are feminine "negative" nature…..93
3-45. True Self-discovery is to discover SHINSEI…..95
3-46. Excessive desire consciousness and the brain dominating structure…..97
3-47. The 5 conditions for spiritual evolution…..99
3-48. The blind spot of the Mobius loop of "vertical love" and the core of ONSHU…..101
3-49. Love and ONSHU between parents and children have distorted the sexual differentiation…..108
3-50. The blind spot of the Mobius loop of "horizontal love" and the core of ONSHU of brothers and sisters…..111
3-51. The blind spot in the Mobius loop of "horizontal love" and the core of ONSHU of husband and wife…..113
3-52. The 21st century is the creative era of spiritually wise women …..120
3-53. Horizontal love of the Mobius loop and integration of sexuality …..124
3-54. Pair system of love in the SHINSEI unity…..127
3-55. History has been built with the love and ONSHU of women …..129
3-56. Chakras are "spiritual organs" to integrate the soul and the body…..134
3-57. Release of chakras and spiritual dimensions…..140
3-58. Dysfunction of chakras occurs by unpleasant feelings…..143
3-59. The time required for disembodiment and spiritual dimensions …..146
3-60. Chakra adjustment methods of resuscitation by Self-reliance and reliance upon others…..148
3-61. The level of releasing chakras determines the direction of

spiritual dimensions…..150
3-62. Verification of sexual integration and sexual anomaly…..153
3-63. The methods to surpass and transcend sexual anomalies…..156
3-64. Chakras will disappear in the "intangible world"…..157
3-65. The relative wave based on the spiritual dimension and the "principle of the relative original power"…..159
3-66. Power of the collective consciousness by the relative original power…..162
3-67. The relative original power and "Surprising phenomena"…..164
3-68. The purpose of the true spirituality formation by Self-completion…..166
3-69. The principle of the relative original power based on the higher dimensional spirit and mind…..168
3-70. Culture and civilization based on spiritual dimension…..171
3-71. Energy waves in the 7 spiritual dimensions…..175
3-72. SHINSEI (true sense) is the common denominator of the entire universe…..177
3-73. The relative original power with the high-dimensional being …..180
3-74. Unpleasant feelings are caused by spiritual disorder…..183
3-75. The way of life to integrate individual purpose and entire purpose…..186
3-76. Create the path to manifest SHINSEI (true sense)…..187
3-77. Advent of "the Eschatology" in Christianity and "the declining days of this world" in Buddhism…..190
3-78. "The Eschatology" in Christianity and "the declining days of this world" in Buddhism, based on the view of religious history…..193
3-79. The sacred revelation from the universe…..196
3-80. Human being is a cancer cell of the terrestrial life entities …..200
3-81. The relative wave and the relative original power based on mind and spirit…..204

Chapter 3

The Turning Point

Chapter Three ☆ The Turning Point

3-1. Limit of the finite theory of the universe

Now, let's turn our attention to the universe. Whether there is an end to the universe or not is unknown and is the eternal theme for us, so at least we can examine the size of the universe within the extent of our knowledge. For example, if we say the sun is the size of a basketball, the earth, located about 10 meters away from the sun, would be slightly smaller than a pea, which means 33 million earths would equal the same mass as the sun. Pluto exists 100 meters away from the sun, so we can imagine just how vast this solar system is.

The galaxy is made up of 200 billion solar system of this size and "the island universe" is formed by gathering hundreds of billions of galaxies, and finally, a part of the continent of the large universe is formed by gathering hundreds of billions of the vast island universe, so that the boundless universe is beyond our imagination.

Ultimately, where is the end of the universe? In contrast, how small can a substance be? The world of microscope is endless. For instance, there is a body and the organs, the tissues and the cells, the molecules and the atoms, the elementary particles and, the top quark, etc.

3-2. Universe is the perfect collaboration

The PARAREVO theory considers the most important is the rule of *"the relative universal original power,"* which affects equally to all things existing in the universe based on free intention, so it is important to clarify what kind of mechanism produces the rule of power and what kind of system makes the rule of function.

Chapter Three ☆ The Turning Point

The PARAREVO theory considers that the power of the boundless universe is basically not directed toward disharmony and disorder. If it is, the universe would have already Self-destructed. Since the earth was born as the third planet of the solar system 46 billion years ago, it continues to spin an orbital rotational motion at a constant speed without any discord at all. If the rotation speed increases, it might go out of orbit and become dust in the universe, or if the rotation speed decreases, it might be absorbed by the sun and be burned up.

An invisible but great power that makes it possible to be relative with innumerable asterisms which exist in the boundless universe, including the earth, and directs the harmony and order without defect and operates perfectly. The PARAREVO theory defines this source of the fundamental power as *the "relative universal original power."* In the Universe, all things are able to be relative by "the relative universal original power" as the common denominator, making it possible to exist from each spiritual dimension to the material dimension.

So, what kind of function and nature does the invisible and great "relative universal original power" have? By looking at all things existing in the universe, we can catch a glimpse of the real nature essence of the fundamental power of "the relative universal original power." All things existing in the universe are carried through by the "rule of freedom" and based on love.

There must be an existing purpose for all things in the universe, and that purpose is to complete the existing value which finds joy toward every object based on free love. The source of power based on free love is the fundamental nature of the "relative universal original power." The entire universe functions to complete the role and responsibility for the existing purpose and to discover the existing significance and value which exists for others based on love, according to the "rule of freedom."

This proves that there is nothing existing for itself in the universe. It needs the "two-way system" of power called "interactive system," that makes it possible to sustain the relative original power in the relative relationship. By this power, it has created the system which makes it possible to exist eternally. So, the "one-way system" is impossible because there is no power which causes the direction of invisible influence and intention to complete its existence.

3-3. "Relative universal original power" and proof of relativity of the universe

Today, the concepts of the universe for space engineers have changed significantly. Through the astronomical observation for the mechanism of supernovae and galaxy far in the distance, the concept which *the universe is manipulated by two kinds of invisible darkness* has become a mainstream idea in the field of astronomy. Those two kinds of darkness seem to be responsible for the driving force of the formation of the universe, so in order to characterize the darkness, astronomical observations have been actively conducted.

One of the darkness is the existence of a mysterious matter called *dark matter*. This existence is impossible to observe with a telescope because it does not produce light or radio waves and does not reflect. Dark matter is considered to have mass density several times greater than normal matter and *gravitation* to attract other

Chapter Three ☆ The Turning Point

things around it. It is known that the rotational speed of the central part and the periphery part is almost the same in the disk-shaped galaxies like the Milky Way where our solar system exists.

If there are only visible stars, the speed of the outer edges of the stars could be much slower. If it rotates at the same speeds, it will cause theoretical contradiction unless there are existing massive quantities of matter which have a mass, called *a halo region,* extending outside of the galaxy. However, in reality, in the halo region, there is only the world of invisible darkness. So, unless we assume that the dark matter exists in the halo region, we are not able to explain the mystery of the galactic rotation.

A US and European international team once made a three-dimensional map that showed how the zone of dark matter has changed in the last eighty million years. They estimated it with a clue of the phenomenon called *gravitational lens effect* by combining the observation of the Hubble Space Telescope and the Subaru Telescope. And they confirmed that no less than five hundred thousand galaxies have overlapped nicely with dark matter, and have existed by creating a large foam like structure. The dark matter is very mysterious. One theory is that it is *super-symmetric particles* which are beyond the standard model of particle physics.

Another and more mysterious existence is *dark energy*. It does not have opposite mass to dark matter, but has *repulsion* which pushes the surrounding matter away. The existence of this energy has been clarified because in 1998, plural supernovas were moving away from the earth at an unexpected speed. With much speculation, the consensus was this energy seemed to accelerating the expansion of the universe starting approximately 90 billion years ago. This consensus overturned the assumption that the expansion speed of the universe has been slower after *the big bang,* 137 billion years ago. This means that depending on the strength of dark energy, the fate of the universe would ultimately be affected whether it would expand eternally, or whether it would shrink.

If the entire universe is converted to energy, the proportion of all things existing is, normal matter only 4 %, and dark matter 27 %, and dark energy is overwhelming 69 %. There is a theory that dark energy is the one inherent in space itself, but unfortunately we cannot explain this using present physics. This is the current astronomy assumption.

Now I will explain the mechanism and system of the universe by the cosmological evidence based on the PARAREVO theory:

In the entire universe, there exists the gravitation that directs to restraint and inconvenience by dark matter, which is the tangible substantial world, and an opposite exists, which is the repulsion that directs to release and freedom of dark energy, the intangible substantial world. Those two powers derive synchronically and contradictory, and disappear at the same time, based on the "rule of entropy relativity," and also exist by forming harmony and order according to the "rule of balance."

Dark energy, which exists all over the universe, is the qualitative energy which is possible to be relative to the spiritual consciousness entity of all levels of spiritual dimensions, and I define this source of power as "the relative universal original power." From this intangible source of power, there are nebulae and planets which are the presence of tangible quantitative energy of the universe, and those are manifested in accordance with the "rule of balance" based on the

Chapter Three ☆ The Turning Point

"*rule of entropy relativity.*"

Like the color black, which comes from integrating all the colors in this world, dark energy occurs when integrating all energies in the universe. By lowering the wave of this qualitative energy, dark energy, it becomes granulated to "super-symmetric particles," and dark matter is formed by an intermediate process leading to the materials. By lowering the energy wave further, by compressing it, it is changed to qualitative energy and materialized.

So, *I define the nature of all quantitative energies in the entire universe, from dark matter to material existence, as the universal original power.* All things in the universe make existence possible according to each spiritual dimension by the power and energy derived by the "relative universal original power." Thus, *the source of power that is possible to be relative to the consciousness entity connoted in all spiritual dimensions existing in the entire universe is called the "relative universal original power."*

For example, assume the Tokyo dome (about 5 ha.) as the whole universe. When compressing and immobilizing all the air inside, it will be converted into solid material that is an infinitesimal amount of quantitative energy, and the whole inside of the dome will become a vacuum. However, it does not mean that the energy itself is lost, so in this vacuum condition, extremely vigorous and high-dimensional free energy appears. The things converted to solid materials are tangible nebulae and stars of the universe. The vacuum world is equivalent to the world of dark energy that occupies most of the universe. The world granulated in the middle position is the world of dark material called dark matter. A black-hole is the nuclear fusion critical substance that "the relative universal original power," the intangible qualitative energy, is relativized and further compressed and granulated, so the mass is compressed up to immediately before the critical stage.

When the air existing in the entire Tokyo dome, as well-balanced, expanding becomes a lump of small substance, the mass balance in the entire dome will significantly breaks, so that the dome will need to keep the entire balance by releasing the entire space balance, expanding by making it free, and inflating it by dimensional ascension of itself, according to the "rule of balance." This phenomenon supports the "rule of entropy relativity," in order to form harmony and order of the "intangible substantial world" and the "tangible substantial world," and the opposite things appear and disappear synchronically and simultaneously making it possible to sustain existence itself.

Therefore, every time a star is born in the universe, the space expands, and the whole universe increases with dimensional ascension and forms a new universe. I would say that the world of dark energy is much bigger than the one that astronomers have calculated, and it is no exaggeration to say that it occupies almost the entire universe.

The "relative universal original power" is the source of power that makes the entire universe possible to be relative and exists as the common denominator of the nature connoted universally. All things are relativized, and like a body of the same root, the entire universe becomes network, *and makes it possible to exist according to each spiritual dimension,* based on the cosmological evidence.

17

3-4. SHINSEI (true sense) and the "rule of original creation power" in the universe

What is the basis of the "rule of original creation power" which created the intangible substantial world and the tangible substantial world in the universe?

The PARAREVO theory describes this rule as follows. *SHINSEI (true sense), which is the spiritual consciousness entity of the intangible substantial world, had been forced to create the opposite tangible substantial world and exist in the universe synchronically and simultaneously, based on the motivation to obtain the object for joy inside itself, by exercise of the subjective consciousness with the impulse emotion of love which tried to obtain joy as the cause.* It means that increasing entropy of the intangible substantial world in which the energy wave becomes free, and decreasing entropy of the tangible substantial world in which the opposite energy wave becomes restraint, appears synchronically and simultaneously by the "relative original power," based on the "rule of entropy relativity."

All things existing in the entire universe have SHINSEI as the common denominator which is the "relative universal original power," and each molecule has individuality and directs to "SHINSEI integration world" and becomes networked by the "principle of dimensional integration." This occurs by a slight fluctuation of imperfection between subject and object in each spiritual dimension. So, as a result, it is possible for the entire universe to exist by forming harmony and order.

If SHINSEI, the common denominator with the potential to be relative to the entire universe is not contained in each entity, the network would not be formed and the harmony and order in the whole universe would be destroyed. Thus, the entire universe is like "a body with the same root" with SHINSEI and being directed to "SHINSEI integration world." By the "relative original power," which occurs between the fundamental "relative universal original power" based on free love of SHISEI, and SHINSEI which is connoted in all existing things in the entire universe, individual molecules become networked and are directed harmonically and orderly, and make it possible to sustain existence.

The "SHINSEI integration world" based on the PARAREVO theory is this. *The entire universe stretches the "SHINSEI integration world" like a network system, all over the universe by making SHINSEI of "the verity of the individual entity" as an individual denominator and SHINSEI of "individual mental entity" as an individual molecule. So, each of us is the individual mental entity and part of the universe. The entire universe existing continuously by directing harmony and order to a higher level produces eternally sustainable power and energy at all times.* There is no concept of time axis in the universe. SHINSEI and the universe are like Alpha and Omega, the beginning and the ending, the cause and the effect, and the subject and the object, so they are the "relative opposite presence."

The "rule of the original creation power" based on the PARAREVO theory is this. *The universe forms the balance by the "rule of the relative original power" caused by a slight fluctuation of imperfection between the relative subjective and the relative objective in each spiritual dimension based on the "rule of entropy relativity." It also completes the objectivity of destruction and the subjectivity of creation (both appear and disappear at same time synchronically and*

Chapter Three ☆ The Turning Point

simultaneously) in the zero time period according to the "principle of dimensional integration," and makes it possible for them to sustain generation and development, eternally.

So, firstly, *the cause and the effect derive the sustainable energy in zero time, as now, by the "relative original power" caused by the slight fluctuation of imperfection between the relative subjectivity and the relative objectivity, and the cause and effect are directed to a higher level according to the "principle of dimensional integration," and are operated evolutionally by deriving and destroying the creation and the destruction synchronically and simultaneously.*

Secondly, *since there is no distinction, time difference, distance, or separation between the cause and the effect, they are perfectly relativized, and directed to being comprehended and integrated to a higher level, making completion.*

Thirdly, *all things connote the cause and the effect inside themselves, synchronically and simultaneously, and are directed toward Self-determination, Self-responsibility, and Self-completion, based on the "rule of freedom."*

Between SHINSEI and the universe, SHINSEI is the relative subjectivity and the universe is the relative objectivity, so that SHINSEI and the universe exist from the beginning, synchronically and simultaneously, by the "relative original power," and are directed to form harmony and order of a higher level by the "principle of dimensional integration" in a slight fluctuation of imperfection. Because of this imperfect fluctuation, creation and destruction are repeated and making harmony and order to direct to a higher level. SHINSEI and the universe are not the absolute and not the perfect existence. Their existence is possible by "the relative original power" of the slight fluctuation of imperfection.

According to the creation of the world in the Old Testament based on earth logical evidence, the God had created the universe over seven days, so that there is a time axis and the cause and the effect exist. There are separation view and distance between God and the universe, and there is clearly a differentiated separation of the absolute God and the whole creation world as object. Therefore, the God which was created by monotheistic view (only one unique and absolute God) does not exist. The view of separation, distance and time axis have created a dependable crutch called *the intangible absolute idol worship of God,* and induce all consciousnesses to hallucination and illusion of the time axis, which is the past relic called the Bible, and the other scriptures.

With the theoretical framework and values of the time axis, our history has been buried in the prison of religious domination, and tied our consciousness to the past and future, and continued to strengthen dependence and domination. Since God, the Bible, and the other scriptures are made by humans, they are not created by the universe, so we do not have any problem living in this world, whether they exist or not. It is understandable that humans are directed to dependence toward religions and shift responsibility, but we should realize that everything is caused due to wrong understanding and ignorance about the view of God.

3-5. SHINSEI is not the only and absolute existence

As I explained earlier, *SHINSEI is the source of power that is able to be relative with the consciousness entities of all things for*

Chapter Three ☆ The Turning Point

every spiritual dimension in the entire universe, and this power is also called the "relative universal original power."

By the causal power derived or created in each spiritual dimension from this "relative universal original power," SHINSEI, of the consciousness entity connoted in the whole creation world of the entire universe, the existence of all things becomes possible, from lower dimension to higher dimension. SHINSEI itself is not an exception, and makes existence possible by "the relative original power" with relative whole creation world, the universe.

Since SHINSEI is not monotheism, expressions such as "pray to God" or "interaction with God" using the word in religions is not right, and moreover, I should say, it is fundamentally wrong.

"Praying" is our consciousness world of idea and concept that is derived by "the relative original power" between SHINSEI (the relative universal original power) and the sentiment world of ourselves connoted in our spiritual consciousness entity, drawn by the exercise of the consciousness in our spiritual dimension. So, it doesn't matter whether it is a God of monotheism or image of Buddha in Buddhism, they are all only objects. The role and existence means of objects are only the exercise of our consciousness based on "the relative original power," but nothing else. Therefore, SHINSEI does not answer to nor interact with prayer in order to guarantee the "rule of freedom." "Inner prayer by oneself" or "inner conversation with oneself" is the correct understanding and interpretation.

All things are drawn by "the relative original power" from one's own SHINSEI and the cause of consciousness in the spiritual dimension, and by exercising the consciousness, we will act and speak based on the motivation. Since the "soul mind" and the "body mind" are unconditionally accepted to exist by SHINSEI, all consciousnesses exercise beyond good and evil with each spiritual dimension by one`s own inner SHINSEI.

SHINSEI of the intangible substance and the universe of the tangible substance produce "the original creation power" in each spiritual dimension, and make it possible to sustain generation and development. SHINSEI has the mechanism and the system necessary for growing and sustaining itself eternally, by enabling itself to make the relative exchange between the subject, love and happiness, and the object, based on "the relative original power" by free love.

Since absolute is only a word, and all things exist relatively according to the spiritual dimension, the rule of freedom works. So, it is not the unique and absolute "one-way" creator, such as monotheism based on the earth logical evidence, but all things existing in the universe make it possible to exist interactively in the spiritual dimension based on the cosmological evidence. Because no power or energy would be produced without relativity, the vector of SHINSEI constantly forms the place of relative and interactive bi-direction, not to the absolute one way direction.

Here is my conclusion. "The rule of the original creation power" based on the cosmological evidence is that *the source of power of the whole universe is not a unique and absolute existence of God, but the relative original power itself that derives in the slight fluctuation of imperfection between SHINSEI, the relative subjectivity, and the universe, the relative objectivity.*

3-6. The views of God dispelled by the PARAREVO theory

Since SHINSEI is also the relative existence in the universe, it exists for the completion of its role and responsibility as the subject of the whole purpose, and completes the role and the responsibility of the individual purpose of the universe which is spiritual individuality according to the level of each spiritual dimension. In the universe, there is no existence of disharmony or disorder; there is only intention to form the collaboration in each spiritual dimension by directing to complete co-existence, mutual prosperity, symbiosis and co-promotion.

The whole purpose of the existence of SHINSEI is *the verity of the individual entity which is the "relative universal original power" based on free love, and individual purpose of the existence of the universe is one`s own individual mental entity which is the "universal original power" of joy*. SHINSEI and the universe are not the existence that considers the unique and absolute *good* as the subject, but are the relative existence of *good* and *evil*.

The universe provides the system that makes opposite things appear and disappear synchronically and simultaneously, according to the "rule of balance" based on the "rule of entropy relativity." In each spiritual dimension, at the moment when the intangible substantial world manifests, the tangible substantial world, as it's opposite, manifests relatively and synchronically. So, God did not create the universe, rather, the intangible SHINSEI and the tangible universe emerged synchronically and simultaneously in the relative dimension.

SHINSEI, the "relative universal original power," provides the system that makes it possible to sustain its own existence eternally by enabling it to be relative to all dimensions in the universe. As SHINSEI accepts the existence of "good person" and "evil person" unconditionally and totally, it also accepts "soul mind" and "body mind" connoted inside us unconditionally, and does not affirm nor deny the existence itself based on the "rule of freedom." This means, never bring in "the theory of good and evil" or "the theory of supremacy."

3-7. Mechanisms of infinity of the universe

Since SHINSEI and the universe are the whole and the individual, the relative dimension spreads unlimitedly, and contains the sustainable mechanism which derives the infinite "relative original power," and creates the system which enables it to exist eternally.

In each relative dimension, the subject and the object, according to the "principle of dimensional integration," provide the system which enables it to grow eternally in each dimension, based on the "rule of change by birth and re-birth." For example, at the moment when we achieve the spiritual evolution to a higher spiritual dimension and ascend to a higher dimensional level, the opposite object would appear and become phenomenon, synchronically and simultaneously, in that spiritual dimension level. So, as you can see, the universe forms the infinite spiritual dimension, and creates the subject and the object in the higher spiritual dimension according to the degree of love and freedom. At the same time, it creates the opposite lower spiritual dimension according to the scale of ONSHU and degree of inconvenience.

The universe constantly derives the opposites, expansion and reduction, synchronically and simultaneously in the relative dimension, based on the "rule of entropy relativity," according to the "rule of original creation power" by the "relative universal original power," and continues creation and destruction to the utmost limit.

As a result, the PARAREVO theory has concluded that since our consciousness is infinite, the universe is the existence of the maximum and the minimum, which means there is no end of the universe. Thus, the restriction of consciousness is the limitation, and without restriction, consciousness itself is infinite.

3-8. Imperfection of the relative fluctuation is the driving force for evolution

From the beginning of time, if the power was only directed to one-way, we would not have any "body mind" and there would be no existence of evil. If we keep creating materials unilaterally in our lives, the entropy increases and the earth will become a mountain of garbage, because it breaks harmony and order and will destroy the earth itself. Unless we provide for the destruction system and reduce entropy once we create something, garbage will inevitably continue to increase.

If we are living only in good, are we able to develop ourselves? Probably not, because we will lose the fundamental power to direct to a higher dimension of good, and lose the "relative original power" itself, which is essential for development, and we will stop growing.

Based on the "rule of entropy relativity," there is good and evil inside of good, and as a matter of balance, when the inside good, the relative subject, exceeds the inside evil, the relative object, by the slight fluctuation of imperfection, good becomes priority and manifests. If the balance of good and evil, the subject and the object, collapses and reverses by the "rule of relative conversion," the evil becomes predominant and manifests. So, the direction of power is always left to the "rule of freedom."

Evil is connoted inside good for the existence of good, and it continues in each dimension`s good, from low dimension to much higher dimension, and no matter how high it goes, evil continues to exist in the antipodes by ascending the dimension of good. In other words, because of the existence of evil in each relative dimension, the good is able to upturn for the dimensional ascension by directing the evolution to a higher dimension of good.

In the negative and in the positive, there are always connoted another negative and positive inside of them, and this relative original power of negative and positive derives to direct to a higher dimension of negative and positive, and makes it possible to sustain. Our "soul mind" and good are directed to a higher level of the "soul mind" and the good by SHINSEI, the "relative universal original power," based on the "principle of dimensional integration" by the existence of the "body mind" and the evil, relatively, in each spiritual dimension. When "soul mind" and good surpass and transcend "body mind" and evil, it will be possible to achieve spiritual evolution to a higher spiritual dimension of "soul mind" and good. This universal law is called *the "rule of evolutionary relative original power" based on the "rule of balance."*

The "rule of balance" provides the evolutionary system, generation and development, according to the "principle of dimensional

Chapter Three ☆ The Turning Point

integration" by the "relative original power," based on the "rule of the relative field." So, whether we complete the spiritual evolution according to the relative subjectivity based on the "principle of dimensional integration," according to the relative wave and the "rule of the relative original power" of each spiritual dimension, or we destroy personality according to the relative objectivity based on the "principle of dimensional domination," is left and determined by our free intention based on the "rule of freedom."

The "soul mind" and the "body mind," and good and evil, in the lower dimension exist relatively, as they do in the higher dimension. We all have "soul mind" and the opposite, "body mind", based on the "rule of entropy relativity." There is no such person who only has "soul mind" and not "body mind," not even Jesus or Buddha. This quality of "soul mind" and "body mind," and good and evil, is determined by the level of love in mind and spirit, and the strength of freedom of free intention, in each spiritual dimension.

No matter how high we go in dimension, we always have the existence of "soul mind" and "body mind" in us, according to each spiritual dimension. Even saints always have two opposite minds, and the level of good and evil is determined as being relative to the personality dimension. For example, the "body mind" of an honest person with an admirable character, such as Jesus and Buddha, exists in a much higher spiritual dimension of the personality level of good than the "soul mind" of a poor personality person in a lower spiritual dimension.

We are forced to exist holding conflict and agony, constantly, by the "relative original power" of imperfection between "soul mind" and "body mind," and the fluctuation between relative good and evil. We must complete spiritual evolution to overcome evil and surpass the "body mind," directing it toward good, with our Self-effort, to raise the level of the "soul mind" to a higher dimension for spiritual evolution, by connecting the relative wave with a higher spiritual dimension and create the "relative original power." Since we are provided the system to complete ourselves in each spiritual dimension, with the rule of Self-responsibility, which makes it possible to sustain spiritual evolution, and with this spiritual evolution, we are eternally directed to the level of the higher dimension's "soul mind," and form the harmony and order.

Spiritual beings in the spiritual world exist in the infinite spiritual dimension from the Astral entity ("ghost" plane) to the Causal entity ("enlightened spirit" plane), based on the forming power of the place and the energy wave, by the relative wave in each spiritual dimension and the "rule of the relative original power."

Religions and philosophy deny the existence of "body mind" and stay in the theory of good and evil, however, "soul mind" and "body mind" exist naturally, so "body mind" is the relative and the essential presence required in order to grow "soul mind" eternally. Even though the "body mind" exists, if you do not invoke it by the "relative original power" based on mind and spirit, you could say that it is the same as not. However, if so, the "soul mind" is also not able to be invoked. So, there is an opportunity for spiritual evolution when the "body mind" is invoked. We should examine ourselves and repent to SHINSEI, invoke the SHINSEI integration consciousness by the "relative original power" of SHINSEI and the "soul mind," and make Self-completion to the "soul mind" in a higher spiritual dimension by surpassing the "body mind" and

Chapter Three ☆ The Turning Point

transcending ONSHU.

Even inside SHINSEI, "soul mind" and "body mind" exist and continue to grow by shouldering the role and responsibility by itself to transcend ONSHU, based on the "rule of change by birth and re-birth." This is the reason that nobody can deny the existence of "soul mind" and "body mind," so the religious theory of good and evil only invite struggles and destruction, but cannot solve the issue of the existence of "soul mind" and "body mind."

Here is my conclusion. The entire universe is possible to be relative with *the verity of the individual entity, SHINSEI which is the "relative universal original power" as the common denominator, and with SHINSEI in the individual mental entity existing in all spiritual dimensions in the universe as the molecule.* And the direction of the spiritual consciousness entity which becomes a network, like "a body with the same root" in the universe, direct the individual art of joy based on free love toward a higher spiritual dimension, and make Self-completion of the spiritual evolution by Self-effort according to the "principle of dimensional integration," based on the "rule of balance."

★See diagram "Steps of the Spiritual Evolution" on P.31

3-9. The "rule of preservation by inscription" based on "All worldly things are impermanent"

According to the PARAREVO theory, things existing in the universe never hold the original form nor do they stop for a moment. It is a world of impermanence, and based on the "rule of preservation by inscription," all things appear instantly and disappear instantly.

Steps of the Spiritual Evolution
soul mind and body mind in the spiritual dimension

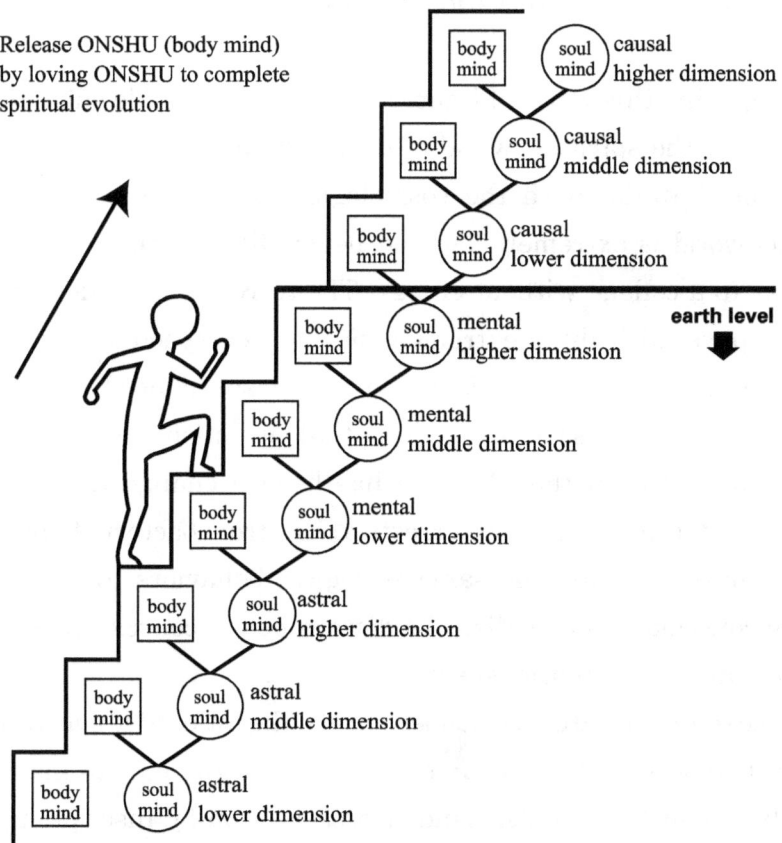

Chapter Three ☆ The Turning Point

Since the world of the spiritual consciousness entity, the intangible substantial world, is a digital presence without time axis, it is always changed with inscription to new information in every second and digitally stored. In this way, the intangible substantial world completes the increase and decrease of entropy in the relative dimension and disappears at the same time, and makes it possible to sustain by overwrite and save new data to a higher level. This is called the "rule of preservation by inscription." (see 3-12 for more details)

Comparing this world of limited analog, the tangible substantial world, and the spiritual world of unlimited digital, the intangible substantial world, with the cosmological view, the energy wave in this world is extremely low and heavy, like an apathetic world similar to a collage without energy. The terrestrial life dominated by the physical body is extremely slow in the speed of evolution, because the energy wave is low and the speed of change with overwrite is slow, so that the spiritual evolution has very slow progress, and even though there has been a change in material shapes and forms, we, as all terrestrial life, from bacteria to human beings have repeated the same ecological behaviors by the same desire consciousnesses called the dietary desire consciousness and the sexual desire consciousness.

Since the spiritual consciousness entity, the intangible substantial world, transcends the time axis, it becomes digitized and makes it possible to sustain by the "rule of preservation by inscription," in which a new dimension is manifested instantly and disappears the moment the energy is released, and completes as free existence. On the other hand, the body, the tangible substantial world, tied to the time axis, becomes analogue by the integral preservation by the brains memories which expanded over the time axis, will be impossible to sustain and will lose everything when the brains memories are lost.

3-10. Physical world benefits and spiritual world benefits are the opposite sides of the coin

Since our spiritual consciousness entity takes the physical domination, we have a tendency to get ideas of things in the tangible world, and make the values by theorizing facts in the physical vision of seeable range with the naked eyes.

Even if all people in the world evaluate a man to be unhappy, if he does not feel any unhappiness by himself and spends every day with gratitude and joy, is he really an unhappy person? Or vice versa, if all people in the world evaluate a man to be happy, is he really a happy person if he feels miserable and spends every day with complaints and dissatisfaction?

If we define true happiness as gaining the physical world benefits such as status, honor and material possessions, saints and righteous persons would seek the excessive physical world benefits. Instead, many saints and righteous persons have been seeking trials and tribulations and hardships by themselves, but none of them sought the physical world benefits.

Seeking the theoretical framework and values of the rule of "body is subjective and spirit is objective" and the rule of "spirit is subjective and body is objective" are directed to the opposite relative values and the reverse vectors according to the "rule of entropy relativity."

Chapter Three ☆ The Turning Point

Physical world happiness does not always lead to happiness in the spiritual world. It is not an exaggeration to say that the spiritual world exists in a rather paradoxical view of happiness. This is the reason for the saying "a rich man going to heaven is more difficult than a camel going through the eye of a needle."

We are able to achieve our spiritual evolution, which is to form harmony and order when we are directed to a higher spiritual dimension, by releasing our own hatred with love to ONSHU, surpassing physical world trials and sufferings by love, based on the "rule of balance" which is derived by the "rule of entropy relativity." ONSHU contains not only hatred but also kind heart, so it means conflict of slight fluctuation between the "soul mind" and the "body mind." Hatred means that the "body mind" overtakes on a large scale.

Since the universe is forced to exist by the "rule of entropy relativity," there is no increase or decrease of entropy in the universe. So at the moment the good arises, synchronically, the opposite evil derives inevitably. It is the same as negative and positive, plus and minus, etc. So at the moment the intangible substantial world occurs, synchronically, the opposite, tangible substantial world derives inevitably, and at the moment life occurs, synchronically, the opposite, death, derives inevitably. It is your decision to exercise the consciousness of the relative subjectivity and use Self-integration, or to exercise the consciousness of the relative objectivity and use Self-domination. In all cases, it is led by Self-determination, Self-responsibility, and Self-completion, based on the "rule of freedom."

3-11. Energy waves in material world and spiritual world

The major difference between minerals, plants, and animals is the speed and the level of free consciousness connoted in each thing. Minerals move the energy wave of their consciousness slowly in the span of millions of years. Since plants have a faster energy wave of the consciousness than minerals, they are able to grow and exist as life entity, but it is impossible to move to a different location by themselves. Animals have an even faster energy wave of the consciousness than plants, which makes life activities and changing locations by themselves possible.

Because the material world, the world of material phenomenon, has the time axis under the material domination, memories and consciousness are preserved analogically and need a great amount of time to grow or move.

The spiritual world does not accept the material domination, so it always preserves memory and consciousness digitally on the zero time limited, now, beyond the time axis and is able to move freely and instantly. So, the more you achieve the spiritual evolution based on the rule of "spirit is subjective and body is objective," surpassing the rule of "body is subjective and spirit is objective," the more the energy wave rises, and your personality (mind) and spirituality (spirit) dimensionally ascend and become free, the pace of free consciousness speed will increase rapidly.

3-12. Memory is always trying to preserve higher inscription

Our memories are unconsciously directed to re-write to new memories. And as a Self-cleansing function, removes unnecessary memories such as unpleasant and sad things, unconsciously, and tries to keep memories of fun and pleasant things as well as necessary things.

In fact, something not worth memorizing is removed within a day from our memories. If memories are preserved unlimitedly, entropy will increase inexhaustibly, and we will be always dominated by memories called illusions and delusions. When the disorderly garbage of memories increase, we are held spellbound and tied to the past and will, mentally and physically, lose integrity. So, it will be difficult to live in the present if we are dominated by past memories, and we will lose the border line between the virtual world (Pretense world) and the reality world (Real world) and will possibly fall into the schizophrenia syndrome. This shows us clearly, that when we are dominated by time axis we eventually fall into Self-destruction.

Strong enmity and resentment make it very difficult for the Self-cleansing function to work, however, eventually time will solve the problem by the "rule of preservation by inscription" and the Self-cleansing system, even though it will take a long time. It might not work in this life time but it will be removed eventually, according to the "rule of reincarnation." On the other hand, we unconsciously tend to preserve the memories of things which give us great pleasure, enjoyment, and strong feelings of happiness. Even though we may suffer from dementia, there is a phenomenon to keep repeating the same things over and over, immersing ourselves in Self-satisfaction and becoming intoxicated with old nostalgic memories, saying those days were wonderful.

Thus, our memories are always overwritten to those of a higher level emotion such as gratitude and joy, by the "principle of dimensional integration" based on the rule of "spirit is subjective and body is objective," and preserved as "the memories of the soul."

3-13. The complex three-dimensional structure of SHINSEI, the soul, and the body

Our life entity is forced to exist and act based on the "rule of the universe." This mechanism and the system are as follows: *SHINSEI and the soul, the spiritual consciousness entity, invoke the consciousness directed to either "soul mind" or "body mind" by the relative wave in the spiritual dimension and the "rule of the relative original power," and are converted to words and/or actions based on motivation.*

Thus, we functionally constitute the complex three layer structure of SHINSEI, the spiritual consciousness entity, and the body, by "the relative original power" in each dimension, and are forced to invoke the consciousness as the life entity, and act based on the motivation. This complex relative original power is called "worldly individual mental entity" or "worldly physical dominating structural entity."

3-14. The definition and the rules of SHINSEI

The definition and the rules of SHINSEI based on the PARAREVO theory are as follows:

First, SHINSEI equally directs to open the path of feeling for all relative things to the joy of a higher dimension based on free love.

Second, SHINSEI accepts the two opposite existing presences based on the "rule of entropy relativity," totally and unconditionally, as they are, and directs them to the relative subjectivity according to the "principle of dimensional integration."

Third, SHINSEI takes all responsibility of the moment, now, as zero time limited, and deletes the information in the lower dimensions based on the "rule of preservation by inscription," and transforms the information to a higher dimension digitally, so it directs the information to a higher level and preserves digitally.

Fourth, SHINSEI connotes the mechanism for the life entity to evolve to a higher spiritual dimension, eternally, according to the "rule of reincarnation" by the "rule of spiritual causality" based on the rule of "spirit is subjective and body is objective," and directs to the system which makes the spiritual evolution possible to sustain.

Fifth, SHINSEI is the source of power that is able to be relative for all dimensions, from lower to higher, and has the mechanism which creates the possible existing relative original power inside itself eternally, and directs all systems to complete with gratitude and joy based on the spiritual dimension.

Thus, SHINSEI, "the relative universal original power," is *the intention power, for the entire universe, which tries to complete the joyful individual art by directing to a higher dimension, based on free love.*

3-15. Spiritual world benefits and physical world benefits based on the principle of freedom

I am able to explain easily, with the PARAREVO theory, about the mechanism of the "rule of reincarnation" and the system in this world which is hard to be explained by religions.

The mechanism of the "rule of reincarnation" is as follows. According to the "rule of physical causality" based on the rule of "body is subjective and spirit is objective," we inherited two major desires, the instinctive survival consciousnesses, in the genetic structural arrangement throughout history. And in order to surpass and transcend this physical desire consciousness, as the assignment in this world, with the "rule of reincarnation" based on the rule of "spirit is subjective and body is objective," we will choose the gene and the parents which are suitable for our assignment by our own spiritual consciousness entity. In brief, by one`s Self-decision based on the "rule of freedom," we will re-birth in this world which aims to the spiritual evolution again.

Then, the memories of the scenario that were drawn in the spiritual world, the intangible earth, are deleted immediately after descent by conception, and based on the "rule of preservation by inscription," they are re-written to new memories at the zero time as now, and the life in this world starts. *Why are the memories in the spiritual world erased? It is because the "rule of freedom" and the "rule of preservation by inscription" function as the first priority. If the life in this world completes according to the memories of the scenario, the "rule of freedom" will be destroyed and lost.*

However, even the memories of the scenario made in intangible earth (spiritual world) are erased, the environment setting in

Chapter Three ☆ The Turning Point

the scenario remains, such as which parents, countries, family conditions, and sex we choose. Especially, it is a very important task in the scenario, to which mother the soul chooses to descend. Because the soul will pick the mother who has similar assignment, you may be able to find your assignment in this world when you inspect your own mother's problems.

The mechanism of generation and development of the universe is referred to your Self-decision, and with your Self-responsibility, you must manage and complete the determination based on the "rule of freedom." So, because you are guaranteed your freedom you have to accept all responsibility by yourself. All mechanism is systemized based on this principal. At the moment the "rule of freedom" is destroyed, the existence of the universe itself will collapse. As long as the universe can use the "rule of freedom," there is the possibility for it to evolve and proceed with its evolution eternally, and generation and development are possible to sustain.

Even in this world, this rule always has priority and all things are directed to this principal. For instance, even though there is a red thread with a marriage partner drawn in the spiritual world, since the "rule of freedom" always has priority it is not necessary to marry exactly as the scenario in the spiritual world. We have the freedom of the right to choose. For example, if you have two options for a marriage partner, one is good-looking, smart and has grown up in a good and wealthy family and highly educated, high income and is a nice young man, and the other is not good looking, has an opposite family background and is an ordinary young man, which you choose is left to your Self-determination based on your free intention, whether it goes with the scenario or not.

We make a future plan for Self-realization and set up our life plan and living plan, but, in reality, I think it rarely goes as planned. Nobody goes through hardships if life all goes well as you planned. This fact is also proven, cosmologically, that since the "rule of freedom" has priority, we make a mistake with wrong Self-determination many times by giving in to selfish desires in the physical world benefits.

The best way not to make a mistake for our Self-determination based on the "rule of freedom" is determined by whether we give priority over the benefits for the spiritual world or the benefits for this world. When we are pressed for the determination for an important choice in life, we should have priority over the advantage for the spiritual world and have courage to dispense with the benefits in this world.

3-16. The "rule of reincarnation" is the curse and bind of instinctive survival consciousnesses

In the universe, all things exist based on the rule of "spirit is subjective and body is objective," and there is no existence without consciousness. The spiritual consciousness entity, which represents the *"intangible substantial world,"* and the body, which represents the *"tangible substantial world,"* exist relatively and oppositely. In other words, all things exist as two sides of a coin by combining the spirit and the substance based on the "rule of relative place."

The difference in both sides is based on the rule of entropy relativity. Just like our soul and our physical body, the earth star exists as the bipolar of two sides, the "tangible substantial earth"

Chapter Three ☆ The Turning Point

and the "intangible substantial earth." In the earth star, the *intangible negative world* and the *tangible positive world* exist as bipolar in a slight fluctuation of imperfection based on the "rule of balance," and in between the two worlds, the tangible atmosphere and the intangible "River" exist, and the whole is integrated to the relative universal original power of the universe.

In the universe, there exist an infinite number of stars with the energy wave in the unlimited energy wave range, which we are not able to confirm by our physical vision. All colors, sounds and created things in the universe are enabled to exist by the proper energy wave. However, like the speed of light oscillates at a rate of about 300,000 kilometers per second, the energy wave range beyond the visible rays exists infinitely in the universe. The bandwidth of energy wave of visible rays in our physical visual range can only distinguish in the wave range of the energy zone from 360 nanometers (NM) to 830 nanometers (NM).

Stars we can see with our naked eye are fixed stars which have been released by the energy wave and have been converted as light by the atmospheric layer and happened to become visible light wave level, so we are only seeing part of the stars. Tangible stars and intangible stars do not exist separately, but exist overlapping each other and being integrated by the spiritual energy wave at a higher dimension. In the universe, stars of various energy zones exist infinitely and interactively as bipolar invisible presence of negative and positive, based on the "rule of entropy relativity" according to the spiritual dimension, from the material dimension to granulated dimension and wave dimension.

The "rule of reincarnation" is the phenomenon that holds

the soul, the spiritual consciousness entity, spellbound by the theoretical framework and value of the "intangible earth star" and the "tangible earth star" and repeats, coming and going in the same category of the spiritual dimension, then descends to the "tangible earth star" from the "intangible earth star" and again going back to the "intangible earth star," repeatedly going back and forth. The reason why such a phenomenon is repeated is because the spiritual consciousness entity is held spellbound by the fated "rule of the genetic chain" of the earth star, according to the rule of "body is subjective and spirit is objective," and is tamed and dominated by the physical dominating structure, and is not able to sweep away the excessive physical world benefits, attachments, and ONSHU (in "body mind" which one's own negative feeling surpasses the "soul mind"), so it remains as the spiritual consciousness entity of a lower spiritual dimension.

Since the primitive life entity was born in the earth star, it had shouldered the instinctive survival consciousnesses as a fate, so that the spiritual consciousness entity, the soul, has been tamed by desires and inconveniences by the physical dominating structure which has been remaining by the genetic domination in the evolutional process of 3.8 billion years, and all terrestrial life, from bacteria to human beings, has been directed by the common desire consciousnesses and has continuously repeated the same ecological behaviors for the physical world benefits, remaining unchanged even though the shapes and figures were different. Therefore, the "rule of reincarnation" will last forever unless the spiritual consciousness entity establishes the true view of life and death based on the PARAREVO theory. We have to have the courage to let the theoretical framework and value of earth level go and release the physical domination by the way of life in PARAREVO, and achieve Self-completion of spiritual evolution up to the cosmic dimension.

3-17. The "rule of relative conversion" in the qualitative world and the quantitative world

All things existing in the entire universe are able to exist according to *the relative wave in the spiritual dimension and the "rule of the relative original power,"* and are composed by the complex of the "intangible substantial world" (consciousness world based on SHINSEI) based on the qualitative dimension, as the subject and cause, and the "tangible substantial world" (phenomenon world based on things and events) based on the quantitative dimension, as the object and effect. Thus, the complex structural forms exist by being directed in one of two ways. One way is by being integrated by the rule of "spirit is subjective and body is objective" and making the qualitative world as the subject and the quantitative world as the object. The other way is by being dominated by the rule of "body is subjective and spirit is objective," making the quantitative world as the subject and qualitative world as the object.

The energy wave of the qualitative world directs to freedom and releases as a vector, and based on the "rule of the entropy relativity," the opposite things appear and disappear synchronically and simultaneously in the slight fluctuation of imperfection, and according to the "rule of dimensional integration" they direct to the relative subjectivity and are completed and operated at the zero time limit.

The energy wave of the quantitative world directs to inconvenience and restraint as a vector, and based on the "rule of increase and decrease in entropy," it is preserved materially according to the time axis domination, and based on the "principle of the dimensional domination," it directs to the relative objectivity and is accumulated in the time axis and operated. By compressing and making the quantitative energy, the spiritual wave, inconvenient, it becomes quantization (elementary particle and top quark) and granular, and furthermore, by making granular material more inconvenient by compressing, it becomes materialized (atoms, molecules) and converted into quantitative energy.

This is the mechanism of process from intangible to tangible. I will explain this as physical phenomenon to make it easier to understand. When cooling down a gaseous body, which is free energy, and converting and compressing to force it to inconvenient restraint energy, it will be changed to fluid (water), and by making atom and molecule inconvenient by further cooling and compressing, it will be materialized as ice. Conversely, when compressing the material, the quantitative energy to the limit, the energy wave will become quantization, and be converted to a huge amount of heat and quantum, and released to the qualitative energy and become a tremendous amount of free energy, which is the "principle of nuclear fusion." The released qualitative energy wave compressed and quantized again by the relative original power with the energy wave in the place of the earth star, it becomes materialized and converted to the quantitative energy.

Thus energies repeat the relative reaction called "inconvenience

Chapter Three ☆ The Turning Point

and restraint" which are contrasted with "freedom and release," simultaneously, and are preserved regularly according to the rule of entropy. This natural principle is called the "rule of energy conservation" or the "rule of mass conservation." Since qualitative energy and quantitative energy are converted mutually and preserved regularly, unless we achieve the spiritual evolution by the dimensional ascent for the spirituality which is the qualitative energy, we eternally repeat the system to go to the earth star of the "intangible substantial world" from the earth star of the "tangible substantial world," and again re-descend to the earth star of the "tangible substantial world" according to the "rule of reincarnation."

3-18. The "rule of reincarnation" of the quantitative world on the earth star

The "rule of conversion" for qualitative energy and quantitative energy manifests as follows. Using iron as an example, the qualitative energy determines the nature of intangible iron as a cause, and then the result of material form, quantitative energy called iron, manifests. So, the intangible nature of aluminum configures the shape of aluminum, also nickel is only nickel if the nature is nickel even if it is plated it with gold. The qualitative energy, which determines intangible nature, also determines the nature of the material and manifests as formalized quantitative energy. So, for instance, even if we completely burn the quantitative energy of iron, changing it from solid to liquid and gas, and release and scatter the energy into the air, we are not able to erase the qualitative energy, which determines the nature of iron, by burning it with the quantitative energy of physical fire.

According to the "principle of dimensional domination," the qualitative energy always becomes low-dimension with the low-dimensional energy wave of the earth star, by the relative original power, and will be restored to the quantitative energy, and then will appear again materialized as iron. So, unless the qualitative energy ascends according to the "principle of dimensional integration" by the "rule of entropy relativity" based on the rule of "spirit is subjective and body is objective," it will be restored to the quantitative energy and repeat reincarnation. This phenomenon is called the "rule of reincarnation in the quantitative world." Thus, no matter how much we use petrochemical energy, it will never vanish from the earth. Instead, it will continue to exist and be restored somewhere. We cremate the body, which is low dimensional quantitative energy, at the crematory, but we are not able to burn the soul, which is high dimensional qualitative energy, by fire in this world.

If the soul, the spiritual consciousness entity, accomplished the spiritual evolution and was released from the physical domination, and ascended to a higher spiritual dimension, like the "causal plane," it would never descend again to the earth star as a prisoner shouldering the physical body, and never again comply with the "rule of reincarnation." However, if the soul, the spiritual consciousness entity, remains the lingering attachment and ONSHU by the physical fixation or obsession to this world, it would be Self-trapped in the theoretical framework and values of the earth star, and will descend again to this world as a prisoner shouldering the physical body by the relative original power and the energy wave of the earth star, according to the "rule of reincarnation" based on the "principle of dimensional domination."

3-19. The qualitative world and quantitative world are reverse vector

We human beings are the same as the universe. According to the qualitative energy, which corresponds to each sentimental world and personality dimension, we will determine our life sentiment and the concept of the way of life, then fix on the behavior of our physical body, which is quantitative energy. Lower ranked human beings with crude and greedy minds, in the lower spiritual dimension, have stronger material desire and domination desire and prefer a luxurious and high profile life style. On the other hand, people with rich and fulfilled minds, like righteous persons or saints, prefer a simple and plain life.

So, as you can see, the qualitative world and the quantitative world always direct to the opposite vector. This qualitative world is called the spiritual world and the quantitative world is called the material world. In the qualitative world and the quantitative world, there exists the spiritual dimension and the physical dimension.

For the "rule of the relative original power" based on the mind and soul, strictly speaking, there are two different relative original powers existing. One is based on the internal factor and the other one is based on the external factor. The first one is the evoked consciousness derived from the relative original power of the mind and the soul residing in you, based on your personality formation history and spirituality formation history, and the second is the evoked consciousness derived from the relative original power of the mind, based on your own personality formation history and the spiritual entity which exists outside of you. The first one is more direct, causable, and inevitable, and the second one is more indirect, resultant, and accidental.

Exercise in normal consciousness and various emotional outbursts and motivations in human relationships are derived from the relative original power based on the internal factor. For instance, even though you don't have any direct involvement, there is always that person who is incompatible, disgusting somehow, and hard to deal with. On the other hand, there is the person with whom you are compatible, have good feelings about, and seems dear to you.

We are experiencing those unpleasant and/or good feelings toward other persons, unconsciously, on a daily bases. The cause of these phenomena exists not in this world, but in the memories of the soul in a past life based on the spirituality formation. There have been repeated relationships of mutual aid of love, such as, one was a murder and one was a victim, or vice versa, and those feelings come up in your subconscious by the relative original power based on the internal factor.

Those feelings are evoked by the relationships of harmony or antagonism, creativity or destruction, and are mostly created as a cause by the relative original power based on the internal factor. Thus, the equation, "our ONSHU ("body mind") is released by loving the ONSHU" exists.

The relative original power based on the external factor works this way. For example, the person who wishes to commit suicide or murder in his sentiment world, and the spirituality entity of the poor

Chapter Three ☆ The Turning Point

spiritual dimension filled with ONSHU which already committed suicide or murder, create the relative original power based on the external factor, accidentally or intentionally, by the relative wave based on the mind and the spirit, then the consciousness was evoked by the motivation and made actions such as suicide or murder. Since the poor spiritual entity leaves the person after he committed murder, because it has accomplished its purpose, so the moment the relativity is cut, the person comes to "his senses" and quickly runs away from the scene.

The relative original power based on the external factor is obviously dependent on your Self-consciousness, and sometimes it is evoked temporarily, or accomplishes totally, each time. For instance, people have an accident unexpectedly, or get an injury or illness suddenly when they become relative with the haunting ghost of their consciousness. Our consciousness is never evoked by itself. *Each personality is created by the "rule of the relative original power" based on the mind and the spirit, either from inside or outside spirituality entity, in some spiritual dimension, and our behaviors are determined according to the motivation by the evocable consciousness.*

As I mentioned earlier, since the mind is derived from the personality formation history and the spirit is derived from the spirituality formation history, you are able to know the external spiritual entity behind another person, and the inner level of the soul in the internal spiritual dimension of yourself, which is the result of the history up to the past life consciousness through the words and deeds of the person.

In the "rule of the relative wave and the relative original

power based on the mind and the spirit," there are two relative original powers existing. One is based on the internal factor under the unconsciousness and the other is based on the external factor under consciousness, so it appears that the results of the personality formation history and the spiritual formation history will be manifested both in internal and external relatively as the consequence. However, in any event, the base of relativity for the relative original power based on the mind and spirit is left to the sentiment world and the personality dimension based on the personality formation history in this world. So, I could say that the most important thing for you is to make the Self-effort to improve the personality dimension by expanding the sentiment, and to ascend the spiritual dimension.

When certain channelers, mediums and fortune-tellers who belong to particular religious groups are saying things, it is actually equal to "a dialogue with themselves." So, they tell the presence of the consciousness based on the spiritual dimension of themselves, like a mirror of their mind, and it is not more or less than that. *It is because the causality and the subjectivity for all words and deeds are connoted inside each person and not anywhere else.*

The "rule of the universe" and the "rule of the earth" are systematized in paradox, so, in the material world material falls from top to bottom unconditionally by gravity, however, in the universal space of zero gravity, material does not move either up or down.

In the spiritual world, the "intangible substantial world," based on the "rule of freedom," your behaviors are by your own decision and you must take full responsibility by yourself in order to guarantee freedom, so that the universe has the mechanism to make spiritual evolution possible to a higher spiritual dimension, and has systematized all things to be guaranteed equally. The universe guarantees freedom and equality, and in return, it is asking for the assurance of the principle of Self-responsibility. If the presence of a higher spiritual dimension intervenes or intrudes in a lower spiritual dimension, arbitrarily, it would be against Self-determination, Self-responsibility, and Self-completion for generation and development based on the "rule of freedom," and it would destroy the harmony and order of the universe.

Therefore, the spiritual entity in a higher spiritual dimension would never intrude or intervene in the life entity on the earth, lower spiritual dimension, arbitrarily ignoring the "rule of the universe." Moreover, according to the "principle of dimensional integration," a person who had experienced love in a higher dimension would never seek love in a lower dimension. A soul which had experienced life as a human being would never want to be a cockroach or ant.

However, because of the "rule of the relative original power" based on the mind and the soul, sometimes an evil spirit in the lower dimension intervenes arbitrarily, using a poor medium or fake angel, for patients with schizophrenia.

3-20. The importance of verifying the spiritual dimension

The spiritual wave is the energy entity and it will be possible to be relative to anything. So, for instance, there are many well-known stories of cursed jewelry, cursed lands or houses, cursed trees or god trees in shrines, evil tigers and bears that attack humans, etc. So, the spiritual wave is able to be relative to minerals, plants, and animals, and it influences humans in various ways.

Some people have an angel`s face, however they actually have a devil`s mind, and some people have a devil`s face but have an angel`s mind, so sometimes if we approach them, easily deceived by appearance and words, we have a bitter experience.

It becomes very important that we verify the spiritual dimension which creates the relative original power by being relative to minerals, plants, animals and human beings.

3-21. The universe directs to dimensional integration

There are three forms of phenomenon in the material world. They are the mineral world as the first Ether plane, the plant world as the second Ether plane, and the animal world as the third Ether plane. They form the material geomorphology in phased spiritual dimensions of the tangible substantial world. These three material geomorphologies systematically form the world of material phenomenon, the quantitative world in the earth star.

According to the "principle of dimensional integration in the universe," the plant world, the second Ether plane, connotes and integrates the element of minerals of the first Ether plane, as it`s component. The animal world, the third Ether plane, completes the operation of animals by connoting the elements of the plant function, the second Ether plane, as the component of formation for each cell, and directs them to dimensional integration. Naturally, the third Ether plane beautifully completes the animal operation by connoting and integrating both the elements of the mineral world and the plant world.

So, as we can see, according to the "principle of dimensional integration," things in the lower dimensions are always comprehended by things in the higher dimensions, and things in the higher dimensions try to direct and integrate things in the lower dimensions to a higher direction so that it will be completing harmony and order and makes it possible to exist. The individual purpose is always directed to the entire purpose. For example, cells are for the tissues, the tissues for the organs, the organs for the whole body. So, individuals are for a family, a family for the ethnicity, the ethnicity for the nation, and the nation for the world. They are trying to complete the existing purpose and the existing values according to the "principle of dimensional integration."

3-22. The PAREVO theory and the equations for spiritual evolution

The fundamental rules of the universe are as follows;

(1) SHINSEI is the source of power which is possible to be relative to the things in all dimensions. This power called "the relative universal original power."

(2) The whole creator world existing in the entire universe contains SHINSEI, the verity of the individual entity, as the nature of the common denominator, and the individual mental entity of each spiritual dimension in the whole creator world as molecule, then forms harmony and order by directing organized network to a higher level according to the "principle of dimensional integration."

(3) SHINSEI and the whole creator world complete the spiritual evolution by repeating integration and domination gradually, according to the relative wave and the "principle of the relative original power" created by the slight fluctuation of imperfection between the relative subjectivity and the relative objectivity in each spiritual dimension.

Therefore, according to those three rules and principles, I can put them together and describe the equation for the spiritual evolution, as follows. *According to the "principle of dimensional integration" by internal separation, we dismiss our "body mind" by directing it to the "soul mind," with SHINSEI as the common denominator, and release our own ONSHU by loving ONSHU, and achieve Self-completion of Self-Enlightenment and spiritual evolution to a higher level.*

By our Self-effort, to practice the way of life of PARAREVO, we can connect the relative wave with a higher spiritual dimension, creating the relative original power with spiritual entity in the higher dimension, and to evoke the subjective consciousness of love and make an action toward all objectives with joy as motivation, then we will be able to achieve spiritual evolution as our Self-completion.

3-23. The criterion of love in the sentiment world determines the 10 levels of spiritual dimensions

Spiritual dimension of the qualitative world is roughly divided into 10 levels by the criterion of love in the sentiment world. For instance, there are three dimensions existing in the "Astral plane,"

Chapter Three ☆ The Turning Point

("the ghost world"). The individual level of the criterion of love in the sentiment world is called the "Astral lower dimension." The criterion of love of family, company, and religious groups is called the "Astral middle dimension," and in the volunteer group level, such as NPO groups which work seriously for contribution to clan and society, is called the "Astral higher dimension."

There are also three dimensions in the "Mental entity." The criterion of love in the sentiment world of the volunteer group level, such as NGO which works seriously for ethnic groups of people, is called the "Mental lower dimension." The level which considers the nation seriously and takes action is called the "Mental middle dimension." The level which considers the world seriously and takes action is called the "Mental higher dimension." The spiritual dimension is determined by expanding territory and contribution of the criterion of love in the sentiment world from individual to family, clan, ethnic groups of people, the nation, and the world.

So, like animals in a zoo, human beings invoke their emotions and consciousness according to their environment, relatively. The person who is only concerned with promotion and relationships in the workplace, his/her own work and financial condition, and his/her own family, or the person who belongs to religious groups and does only missionary work and activities for his/her own religious groups, is the kind of person who put the cart before the horse. In other words, this kind of person has the purpose of life and the goal of life mixed up, and when his/her life is completed, ends in the "Astral middle dimension."

To survive in this world, we also need the physical world benefits. So we should have the real purpose of life, which is Self-completion of Self-Enlightenment and spiritual evolution, and at the same time, we should be considering the individual goal of physical world benefits as the opposite pole, and to establish Self-integration in order to accomplish the role and responsibility of integrated individual purpose.

It is a sad fact, but most people are controlled by the instinctive survival consciousnesses and living their precious life just for an immediate profit in a haphazard way for the life to live for living, even though they know they will die eventually.

It does not seem that government officials, members of Congress, and officials in the foreign ministry, work for the nation and the world seriously with the criterion of real love in the sentiment world. In fact, it is quite the opposite. Most of them are arrogant and consciously dominated by domination desire and material desire as the excessive physical world benefits, such as reputation, status, and material wealth, with values of desire for individual worth. This is the criterion of love in the sentiment world of the spiritual dimension up to "Mental entity" in the earth level.

The "Causal dimension," the world of enlightened spirit, is the spiritual dimension of the criterion of love in the sentiment world which is far beyond the earth dimension. There are also three dimensions in the "Causal entity," and it is the spiritual world which has achieved the spiritual evolution to the consciousness dimension of the universe of the galactic system beyond the universe of the solar system. In the SHINSEI and Spirit world, the "Monad plane" is the territory of SHINSEI integrated life entity and is integrated into a single dimension.

3-24. Gradual stages of the sentiment world in the spiritual dimension

The spiritual dimensions are roughly divided into 10 stages. The "Astral plane," "Mental plane," and "Causal plane" are each divided into three dimensions, and the "Monad plane" is integrated into one dimension.

I can give you an easy guide line to comprehend the spiritual dimension.

The person belonging in the "Astral lower dimension," the spiritual dimension of the poor personality level, has the core of strong ONSHU toward his/her own parents, and is usually a person who committed murder or suicide, criminals in general, communists in materialism, and/or members of criminal organizations. The person who belongs in the "Astral middle dimension" is the person in the religious groups being forced poor creed, dominated by the rule of physical causality, converting its responsibility to ancestors or others by the theory of the original sin or the theory of fate based on victim consciousness, and being threatened to go to Hell when they die if they do not complete the creed in this world, and being restricted themselves by insecurity and fright, such as the person who lives for status, reputation and material, aiming for social success in the central point of desire for excessive earthly benefits, or the person who lives a life for living, only for family with general values. Those belonging in the "Astral higher dimension" are the ones who live in the level of conscience, and could contribute to society by expanding the criterion of love in the sentiment world and would do volunteer activities for society without compensation, with ethics and moral values beyond the religious values, but in the family clan level.

In the "Mental lower dimension" is the person who could expand the criterion of love in the sentiment world for accomplishing the role and the responsibility of the individual purpose to the entire purpose up to the ethnic level, according to a new paradigm of new values, without belonging to any organization or group, transcending the theoretical framework and value of religions and inner space. The "Mental middle dimension" is inhabited by the persons who could expand the criterion of love for accomplishing the role and responsibility of the individual purpose to the entire purpose, up to the nation, by awakening the real patriotism and achieving Self-discovery to find out the meaning and value to choose this nation as a place for this life. Those in the "Mental higher dimension" are the ones who could expand the criterion of love for accomplishing the role and responsibility of individual purpose to the entire purpose, up to the world, by achieving Self-discovery to find out the meaning and value to live this world as the life entity of this planet, and try to find the answer why we have chosen this earth star, the prison planet.

Above the "Causal plane" of the spiritual dimension, of it is impossible to expand the criterion of love with the physical senses and knowledge.

The people who live the way of PARAREVO understand that the purpose of life is a preparation to go to the spiritual world, so that they do not depend on words and knowledge, but create the world of resonance or sympathy with the spirit in a higher dimension inside themselves by exercising of sensitivity and sentiment actively created by the relative original power. The spiritual world is the

Chapter Three ☆ The Turning Point

world which does not require words and knowledge, so people who live the way of PARAREVO are making an effort to not depend on words and knowledge, and aim for the creation of the individual art of joy based on free love as their sentiment world of living.

Words and knowledge contain pretense and deception, but the wave of the life entity and the life are not deceived because it is exuded from inside the person.

In the spiritual world, since things held in the consciousness and thoughts are immediately transmitted to another, so people who live the way of PARAREVO aim for Self-Enlightenment and spiritual evolution. It can heal many people and give peace and calmness, directing to gratitude and happiness by the wave they emit rather than by communication through words.

3-25. The criterion of mind and spirit determines the 10 levels of spiritual consciousness entities

I am going to explain in more detail how we should live our life in order to graduate from the earth star, the prison planet.

The vector of the existence purpose in the universe is this. *The entire universe is integrated by SHINSEI, the relative universal original power, based on free love, and all things are always directed to the "principle of dimensional integration," and exist in the SHINSEI integration world.* Life based on free love suggests the fundamental attitude and direction of the universe, so the practice of the PARAREVO way establishes Self-integration, as now and I, and accept them as they are, unconditionally and totally, with gratitude and happiness, and will guide to Self-completion that is the fundamental individual purpose and the individual value of the universe.

The true purpose of life for all human beings on the earth star is only one. It is to graduate from the earth star eternally by releasing the spiritual consciousness, the soul, from the physical domination structure, the instinctive survival consciousnesses, and direct to a higher spiritual dimension. Also there is one more important requirement to graduate from the earth star. We are not only releasing the physical domination structure, the instinctive remaining consciousnesses caused by the genetic domination, but more importantly we should release the domination structure of the fundamental whole creator world.

Our sentiment world and the personality dimension have stored the sub-consciousness through our spirituality formation history started from the instinctive survival consciousnesses, together with our evolutional process and manifested the emerging consciousnesses by reaching to the personality formation history of this world, so we live in this world with the three layered structure, the triangle system of SHINSEI, the spiritual consciousness entity, and the body.

Through the history of evolution, human beings have directed the spirit world and the personality dimension to graduate from the earth star unconsciously, so eventually we could reach the final stage after climbing the 10 steps of the spiritual dimension, one by one.

The criterion of the formation process of the mind and spirit is derived from the spirituality formation history and the personality formation history, and created by the relative original power based on the internal factors, and formed by each spiritual dimension in the mind and spirit world.

There are 10 vertical levels in the spiritual dimension. The lowest level is the criterion of spirit and mind of "servant of captive." Next lowest is the criterion of spirit and mind of "captive" by oneself, then going up to the criterion of spirit and mind of "adopted child," "illegitimate child," "legitimate child," "mother and father," "the moon," "the sun," "the universe," and the highest level is the criterion of mind and spirit of the "SHINSEI integration consciousness," and according to the relative original power with the relative wave based on each spiritual dimension of 10 levels, we will achieve Self-Enlightenment and spiritual evolution. Thus, we will transcend the physical desires by the love of "soul mind," maturing ourselves, transcending step by step by surpassing ONSHU of each spiritual dimension, with love.

3-26. The 10 levels of the criterion of physical desire

The substantial criterion of desire is to establish the integrity of both the individual purpose and the entire purpose to a higher dimension, by directing the existing purpose and the existing value from individuals to families, clans, ethnic groups of people, nations, the world, the moon, the sun, the universe and "SHINSEI integration life entity," and by expanding the degree of acceptance of love of the relative wave of the spiritual consciousness entity and the degree of freedom of consciousness. By doing so, the relative original power, based on spirit and mind, will derive, according to the "principle of dimensional integration," by responding to each dimension, and achieve spiritual evolution.

In the spiritual world, the criterion of desire to live is explained as the following levels. To live with egoism as the self-centered subject of the individual will be completed to the spiritual dimension of "servant of captive." To live for family will be completed in the spiritual dimension of "captive." To live for clan will be completed in the spiritual dimension of "adopted child." To live for ethnic groups of people will be completed in the spiritual dimension of "illegitimate child." To live for nation will be completed in the spiritual dimension of "legitimate child." To live for world will be completed in the spiritual dimension of "mother and father."

To live as being relative to the moon will be completed in the spiritual dimension of "Enlightened Spirit" (spiritual consciousness entity that extremely defers to "Truth Spirit" with love as intercession) in the spiritual world. To live as being relative to the sun will be completed in the spiritual dimension of "Truth Spirit" (spiritual consciousness entity that practices truth rightfully, and exists according to the truth of the universe). To live as being relative to the universe will be completed in the spiritual dimension of "SHINSEI integration life entity," and by the two layer structure (pair system) of SHINSEI and the spiritual consciousness entity, based on the "rule of spherical theory," it will create eternally sustainable energy and will be internalized into the universal system as the potential existence, by directing generation and development constantly and eternally.

3-27. The criterion of spirit and mind of the 6 stages in the level of the earth

This is the criterion of spirit and mind of the six levels of the spiritual dimension on the earth star.

The criterion of spirit and mind of "servant of captive" stage is explained like this. Looking from the universal dimension, the life entity of the "prison planet" connotes inferior spiritual transformation history and personality transformation history in its spiritual consciousness entity, so it is already the dimension of captive itself. So, the spirit and mind of "servant of captive" stage is the consciousness world of the captive's way of life, who committed crimes and was imprisoned in a real jail on the earth star, and placed in a more inconvenient and poor environment. It is like the patients in hospital who are bedridden and cannot move by themselves, but are forced to live for months and years in the last stage of their life in a condition more inconvenient than prison. It is the spiritual dimension of those who have only built the Self-centered criterion of spirit and mind, filled with frustrations, anger, and complaints.

The criterion of spirit and mind of "captive" stage is the spiritual dimension of those who hold the core of ONSHU in their parent-child relationship, holding a grudge against the parents, and having strong Self-hatred. Those people are often depending on the doctrines and the organizations of religious groups or gangs as a substitute for the parents, shifting their responsibility to parents and ancestors by falling into victim consciousness, being trapped with anxiety and fear because of the organizations or doctrines, being forced by illegal acts or memorial services for ancestors, being dominated and subordinated to the organization or groups, and have an inconvenient and poor life with anxiety and fear, according to the "principle of dependence and domination."

The criterion of spirit and mind of "adopted child" stage is the spiritual dimension of those who had a childhood without knowing love from the biological parents, or raised by poor minded parents who were dominated by the excessive desire and egoism, have being raised with excessive interference such as a mother who is obsessed with her children's education, or raised by obsequious blind love of grandparents because of conflict between mother or father and grandparents. Some of them have a twisted personality transformation history, and become a poor single person who cannot be independent, or a social dropout and NEET (not education, employment or training), and have strong distrust of others.

The criterion of spirit and mind of "illegitimate child" stage is the spiritual dimension of those who have a background and the personality formation history of half brothers and sisters. They often have strong envy and jealousy caused by differentiation of love, and being always conscious of other people's eyes and evaluation, being involved in the physical world benefits such as status, reputation, honor, and materials possessions, valuing appearances and vanity, being always dominated by the "rule of exclusion theory by jealousy," containing Self-hatred and Self-denial, unconsciously conducting Self-injurious activities by unpleasant feelings and losing the existing position of oneself, and living with poor and greedy mindedness, and immorality of selfishness by hypocrisy of Self-satisfaction. The criterion of spirit and mind of "legitimate child" stage is the spiritual dimension of those who have achieved

Chapter Three ☆ The Turning Point

the personality formation history by receiving sincere love from parents, having less internal conflicts, and being satisfied with human love, so that they are able to deal with anyone and are filled with peace and comfort.

The criterion of spirit and mind for "mother and father" level is the spiritual dimension of those who do not hesitate to give their love, and are able to pass the feeling of peace and healing by only being present, and are able to live with great virtues of unselfishness by the charity of Self-sacrifice.

These criterion of spirit and mind are the boundary between the Earth level and the Universal level, and is the boundary which distinguishes from the substantial world with human love according to the physical dominating structure which is the instinctive remaining consciousnesses caused by the genetic domination based on the rule of "body is subjective and spirit is objective" in the earth level, to the spiritual world with universal love based on the rule of "spirit is subjective and body is objective" in the universal level.

In Buddhism terms, this is called the cycle of reincarnation through the six realms of existence and that means from Hell to hungry ghost, beast, Asura, human world and Heaven, however, in the spiritual dimension of the PARAREVO theory, it is fundamentally different. Unless we transcend the boundary, we have to be reborn to this world repeatedly, according to the "rule of reincarnation." No one had transcended this boundary on the earth, not even Jesus or Buddha. However, recently, a Japanese woman who lived the PARAREVO way was released from this rule and beautifully graduated from the earth star and became a spiritual consciousness entity in the star of the higher dimension.

3-28. The equation for "regeneration of SHINSEI and soul"

Spiritual evolution will be completed by being directed to the "principle of dimensional integration." It can't be completed by *the theory of men as the relative objectivity,* just as it is impossible for men to become pregnant and bring a new life to this world. History has already clearly proven that with the religious theories based on *the men's theory of power, domination, struggle, and destruction,* it would absolutely not be possible to complete the spiritual evolution and graduate from the earth star, because men who are the relative objectivity, such as Jesus and Buddha were, could only build a lot of histories of struggle.

Because the equation of spiritual evolution is left to women, the relative subjectivity, and according to the "principle of dimensional integration" based on *the women's theory of love, integration, harmony, and creation,* the evolution for soul and body is going to be done inside the womb, which is a sanctuary for spiritual evolution, based on the "rule of the change by birth and re-birth," with the physical improvement by genetic recombination and the spiritual quality improvement, synchronically and simultaneously, by the "rule of the relative original power" based on the spirit of maternal love.

So, after accomplishing all roles and responsibilities in this world, we are going to the next spiritual world which is outside of the tangible and intangible earth. At that time, according to *the equation of regeneration of SHINSEI and the soul,* spiritual penis (key) and spiritual vagina (keyway) need to be matched. This means that receiving the man's soul to the woman's spiritual womb with love, the man and the woman will be united as a sex integrated life entity when the key and the keyway are matched. Then the spiritual consciousness of women will be re-birthed to a SHINSEI integrated life entity by changing the man's soul by birth to a SHINSEI integrated life entity and re-birthing to a spiritual world of new dimension, synchronically and simultaneously, according to the "rule of the change by birth and re-birth."

Unless our spiritual consciousness entity is integrated dimensionally to "SHINSEII integrated life entity," the spiritual evolution to become a new cosmic life entity will never end, so we will never be freed from the earth star, the prison planet, and the "rule of reincarnation" will continue eternally. No matter how excellent and superior men are, even the righteous and saints, they would never complete love by themselves. The subjectivity of love is given to women and regeneration of life and spiritual evolution are only left to spiritually wise women.

Therefore, in the era of decline, by the Buddhism terms, *the appearance of more spiritually wise women is eagerly awaited.*

3-29. The relative original power with trinity of Sun, Moon, and Earth

The spiritual world beyond the earth star can be self-formed by the relative original power between the tangible and intangible substantial world which are existing outside of the earth. It will be impossible for us to reduce the physical domination, unless we release the physical dominating structure, which is more fundamental than the genetic domination. In order to do so, we must connect the relative wave with spiritual presence of the higher spiritual dimension, which already transcended the earth star, create the relative original power with the spiritual presence, and integrate the body to the spiritual consciousness entity.

The most familiar presences of the universe existing outside of the earth are the sun and the moon. The spiritual energy waves of the moon and the sun are the essential and important energy to transcend the boundary of the spiritual world and the substantial world, and ascend. The energy waves of the moon and the sun are able to raise the relative wave with the earth star, dimensionally, and by creating the relative original power of the higher dimension, make it free by granulating the materials, and forming the light energy. And the reversible response of them will become phenomenon, synchronically and simultaneously, by the rule of entropy relativity. The energy wave of the moon and the sun transcend the atomic level to the level of elementary particle and top quark of the earth star, and give influence to the territory of the dark matter which is ultra-relative particles.

So, you could say that without the presence of the sun and the moon there was no birth or even existence of the life entity on the earth star.

Bacteriophage can exist without the presence of water and air, but all life entities on the earth star will disappear at the moment the moon and the sun disappear. That is, by the transformation energy created by the relative original power between the spiritual energy wave of the moon and the sun as the higher spiritual dimension, and that of the earth star as lower dimension, makes it possible for life entities to exist at the level of the earth star, which shoulder the materials, and it prepares the natural environment for them by converting the energy to essential lights and calorific values. For example, with the presence of water and air, visible light and temperatures are created unlimitedly by the relative original power in the earth`s atmosphere, and the moon and the sun, and it also creates various essential energies in a wider range.

So, the moon and the sun form the natural environment by changing to various energies by the relative original power with the earth, because they supply necessary energies and environment for the terrestrial life entities.

3-30. Substantial "relative original power" with the moon

What is the criterion of spirit and mind of the relative wave of the moon? Here are examples of the role of the moon in the energy wave.

There are incalculable benefits of the spiritual vibration which the earth star receives from the moon. In particular, it supplies the inevitable masculine positive energy of the higher spiritual dimension for women, and gives the sexual balance and hormone balance of women. Since female pheromone is secreted and makes easier to conceive by opening the womb in the full moon, reproductive activity takes place vigorously by the stimulation of male hormones in the animal world.

The moon is often considered as feminine, but it is completely the opposite. The energy wave of the moon conducts all vibration adjustments in the whole creator world in the earth star, and forms the growth, harmony, and order. Therefore, it is possible for our body to exist. Also it is the energy wave of the moon that constantly keeps the ecology in balance in the ecosystem by pouring the energy vibration to the whole creator world, in order for all life entities on the earth star to exist.

3-31 The energy wave of the moon and atomic conversion

In order for the body to grow, the presence of the energy wave of the moon becomes inevitable.

Plants have significant differences in the growth form during the full moon and new moon periods. For instance, timber, in Japan's Nara period (710 to 784) was harvested and buildings were constructed during the new moon period. During the new moon period, all growth stops and no starch is produced, so trees alive in a mummification condition that makes materials clamp firmly together without starch and water, and are not so susceptible to rot or mold. In Europe, it is called new moon timber, and it is said that houses built in the new moon period would last longer. Conversely, timber harvested in the full moon period contains plenty of starch and moisture, so that it is easy to rot and become moldy and will not last long. Full moon period is the growth period, so the trees repeat vigorous cell division in unison and make great strides in growth.

In the animal world, breeding activity and predatory activity increased tremendously, and very different kinds of minerals are produced in the formation of salt during the new moon and the full moon. Although only a dozen minerals are generated in the new moon period, more than 70 different minerals are generated in the full moon period.

This proves that the energy wave of the moon reacts with certain catalysts, and chemical reaction occurs by the relative original power with seawater, and atomic conversion is done in nature without any difficulty. Also it is proof that various chemical reactions occur at the atomic level. It is the paranormal chemistry world of the moon light energy, which transcends, by far, the knowledge level of natural science of human beings.

3-32. The difference of physical effects between the new moon and the full moon

Our body also has a difference of the absorption of nutrients between the full moon and the new moon. During the new moon period, even though we eat foods combined with natural medicines, or healthy and nutritious foods, they will never be absorbed effectively. In order to ingest medicine, healthy food, or nutritious food efficiently, we should take necessary nutrition during the full moon because absorption efficiency is high. So if we want a healthy diet, we should plan to ingest meals according to the lunar cycle. Also, we can lose weight healthily and naturally.

I think that is why the Chinese character of stomach, liver, spleen, kidneys, lungs and other organs has the moon character mostly in the left-hand side. Especially the energy wave of the full moon promotes metabolism of the hormones, adrenaline and dopamine, in the brain, so that brain waves become higher, raising the beta and gamma waves, the immune cells show excitement and then immunity is activated rapidly.

Autistic people or people with schizophrenia also might show suspicious behavior during the full moon, or have sexual delusions or hallucinations, and manifest a noticeable trend to be restless and act incomprehensibly. It is no exaggeration to say that stories of werewolves and Dracula haunting in the night of full moon are occult novels, with subjects about mental disorders, bizarre behavior, and pathological behavior elicited by the energy of the full moon.

By learning the method to take the energy wave of the full moon, correctly, it will be possible to enhance immunity rapidly, and become mentally stable by suppressing undifferentiated sexual desire consciousness. If psychiatry studies more about the energy wave of the moon and how to use it correctly, it will not have to depend on potentially dangerous medicines with side effects and will not have to make unnecessary burdens for patients.

3-33. Possible methods to make energy conversion of water molecules

The crucial difference between the earth star, the prison planet, and other plants is the presence of water. The earth is the planet covered with water. Terrestrial life cannot survive without the benefits of water. Water creates air, air creates the atmosphere, and the atmosphere creates the gravitational field. Because of the gravitational field, terrestrials are equally sealed in inconvenience and forced to exist, which is the fate of lives with physical bodies.

Chapter Three ☆ The Turning Point

Unless we release the physical domination structure, which is more fundamental than the genetic domination, it is impossible to release the physical domination itself in the true sense. Especially, the energy wave of the full moon plays a great role and responsibility for the earth star, the water planet, because the full moon energy makes the molecular structure of water free and activates it creating the physical energy required to live in this world. The molecular structure of water is integrated (or bound) by the ion integration of two hydrogen atoms with a single oxygen atom. The water's molecular structure is oxygen-dominating integration, and it will be a stable molecule when the two hydrogen atoms keep the bond angle of 104.5 degrees with an oxygen atom as the center.

The 104.5 degrees is the basic helix angle in the natural world. For example, the spiral angle of a conch and DNA spiral angle are both 104.5 degrees. When the oxygen domination becomes stronger, the hydrogen atoms are bound and the bond angle becomes narrower, so the activity range of the hydrogen atoms also becomes narrower, and the energy grade of the molecules as a whole will decrease. On the other hand, when the oxygen domination is weakened, the bond force to the hydrogen atoms is weakened and the hydrogen atoms become free and the bond angle is expanded, so that the energy grade of the molecules overall will increase. Since the energy wave of the molecules is determined by the strength of the oxygen domination, this phenomenon is called "the oxygen dominating structure of the water molecules."

Water acts as a guardian of the earth star, and the life entities of the prison planet are directed to inconvenience by the principle of dimensional integration, according to the rule of "body is subjective and soul is objective." Even the water molecules are structuralized by the dominating structure by the triangle system, in which the two units of hydrogen are dominated by one unit of oxygen, and forced to exist by the oxygen dominating structure. By releasing the oxygen dominating structure of the water molecules, making them free, it will be possible to create tremendous energy from the water molecules. This energy is converted into our body energy which means, it also will be possible to take a large amount of energy from water, artificially.

There are two ways to release the oxygen dominating structure of water.

One is to release the oxygen domination by resonance of oxygen and the relative original power of oxygen, and other way is to release by resonance of hydrogen and the relative original power of hydrogen. So, by releasing either compressed liquid oxygen or liquid hydrogen in the water, the synergies resonance (resonance phenomenon) by the relative original power by the relative wave between the oxygen of water molecules and oxygen, or between hydrogen and hydrogen, and making a snowball phenomenon by chain reaction and releasing the oxygen dominating structure of water, it will be possible to take the collapsed energy of water molecules and use the heat converted energy.

If we can take the energy which occurs when water molecules become free, we can use them as safe and clean energy instead of creating a negative legacy, and it will be possible to recur naturally as water, and possible to create energy without limitation. In the near future, cars and airplanes that run by water instead of petrochemical energy will appear on the water planet. In fact, hydrogen-fueled cars have already appeared on the market.

3-34. Dependency on water and the principle of domination

There is no reason we should not use water effectively on the water planet. There are only four elements composing our body system, which are Hydrogen, Carbon, Nitrogen, and Oxygen, and they occupy more than 99% of our body system. And more than 70% of its constituent molecules are water, so that oxygen and hydrogen occupy the greater part. The earth star is constrained by the gravity field of the atmosphere like iron bars, making it the prison planet. Since terrestrial life is dominated (restricted) by the gravity field covered with water, and the body itself is filled with water, the earth star is the planet of life by water domination.

It is no exaggeration to say that since the soul, spiritual consciousness entity, is the life entity dominated by the body filled with water, the fundamental dominating structure, rather than the genetic domination, is actually "the oxygen dominating structure of water molecules." We, as the terrestrial life, are not able to live without water, because if there is no water, even air will not exist. However, ironically, it is also true that we are dominated and bound by water by depending on water, according to the "principle of dependence and domination."

The true release from the physical domination is to release the oxygen dominating structure of water molecules rather than to release the genetic domination. By releasing the oxygen dominating structure of water molecules, the energy ranking of the water molecules will rise by freeing hydrogen atoms, and the physical life energy becomes inevitably active. Therefore, as the physical domination is released, the gap in the energy ranking between the soul, the spiritual consciousness entity, and the body will decrease, releasing the physical domination easily. This is due to the birth of the material world in the universe.

3-35. The world of "SHINSEI integration consciousness" is infinite

The origin of the universe is born interactively, synchronically, and simultaneously, with the spiritual SHINSEI as the relative subject and with the substantial universe as the relative object, by the relative original power with the slight fluctuation of imperfection.

The universe is seen as a totally dark world with the naked eye, because the wave range which can verify with the naked eye in the physical vision is limited, and as I have mentioned many times, the wave range which is the visible rays of naked eye is limited from short-wave wavelength, 360 nanometers, to long-wave wavelength, 830 nanometers. The relative wave range between the relative universal original power in the universe, and the intangible substantial world is composed by the energy wave world called "SHINSEI integration consciousness," that is far beyond the speed of light. The extremely high energy wave, which greatly transcends the wave range of the physical visible light in the physical vision, exists unlimitedly.

The world of "SHINSEI integration consciousness" is the world of spiritual light of spiritual energy wave in which light spectrums are in full play, and filled with love of the higher spiritual dimension, so that the range of the energy wave of the visual light in our naked eye only prepares the abilities with which we can verify the existence in the narrow range equal to nothing in the world of the energy wave existing in the universe. In fact, with our naked eye, not only are we unable to verify infrared light rays and X rays, but also elementary particles such as mu meson, pi meson, and kerma meson, called the universal rays, and electromagnetic waves which are invisible rays.

In the universe, there are universal waves and universal life entities existing, eternally, in the unlimited energy bands. But with the knowledge level of human beings, we will never be able to fully comprehend this. When we human beings verify ourselves cosmologically, we are exactly the same as the blind who do not see anything with their physical eyes. Moreover, I could say that visually impaired people may have seen more things in the universe than people with "normal" vision.

In fact, the organisms that inhabit the bottom of the sea do not need light; however, they actually have eyes and engage in life activities by adapting to their environment.

3-36. The release of the body from oxygen domination

In order for us to graduate from the earth star, the prison planet, we have to release the oxygen dominating structure, which is a more primitive and fundamental dominating structure of water molecules than the genetic domination. So, true liberation from the physical domination is to release the oxygen dominating structure of water molecules rather than to release the genetic domination.

According to the breathing techniques of the PARAREVO theory, when we stop breathing consciously and block the supply of oxygen intermittently, we are able to release hydrogen from the oxygen domination of water molecules and also release the physical domination by freeing the genetic domination. When we do so, the spiritual consciousness entity, which was dominated by the body, becomes the condition of degeneration consciousness for a few seconds, and then it will be possible to see a glimpse of the spiritual world, our reincarnation history, instantly, by recalling memories of the soul. Continuing on this line, when the spiritual consciousness entity completely removes itself from the body, we reach the physical death.

The atmosphere created by water has created a physical barrier called the gravitational field, in order to prevent the body from arbitrarily leaving the earth. Also, spiritually, it has created a spiritual "River" at the border between this world and the spiritual world, and it says that the spiritual consciousness entity, the soul, cannot go to the spiritual world arbitrarily. Many persons who have had a near-death experience have confirmed the presence of the "River," and testified that there was a spiritual world beyond the "River."

Therefore, it is important that we do not neglect the presence of water. Especially, in order to raise the energy ranking of the spiritual consciousness entity, we should free water inside the body and create effective energies, and create the relative original power with the energy wave of the moon.

Chapter Three ☆ The Turning Point

3-37. Hydrogen was the first element in the universe

When the sun and the moon correlate their relative wave with the level of the earth star, they compress the relative original power by lowering the dimension of qualitative potential energy and slowing the speed of the energy wave. By restraining the qualitative energy of the sun and the moon, and making them inconvenient, they will be converted to the quantitative energy and materialized (atoms and molecules) through the process of granulation (particles and top quark).

The energy wave of the sun and the moon are indispensable for the life entities on the earth. The first element to materialize and appear in the universe was hydrogen. Then, lowering the qualitative energy wave and dimension, helium, lithium and beryllium were born, the quantitative energy increased, and large gravity elements that had huge mass numbers and were not free but strongly restricted, appeared.

The freest, least restricted, and light specific gravity element in the universe is hydrogen. So, the hydrogen element is the material dimensional element, which is the closest to the spiritual world, and it is the one existing at the boundary between the "intangible substantial world" and the "tangible substantial world." When increasing the atomic numbers, the material binding becomes stronger, specific gravity becomes heavier, and the quantitative potential energy becomes higher, then the qualitative potential energy becomes lower. Therefore, lower atomic number elements will be dominated and integrated by higher atomic number elements, inevitably.

When an unstable element, which is the transuranic element in an excited state, causes a chain of nuclear decay at once after reaching the critical, all restricted energy is converted to material heat energy or quantum energy, and released after dispersing a new radioactive isotope as a nuclear fragment. The qualitative energy released in the air is again compressed and materialized according to the rule of preservation. This formula has been used for nuclear energy.

The element which connects the relative wave with oxygen the most and derives the relative original power is oxygen. By resonating with oxygen, the restrictive power of the oxygen domination is released. Also by freeing the hydrogen atoms, the energy levels of the water molecules increase and the ground energy wave of the entire body becomes activated. So, this is the reason why the breathing technique becomes an important method of resuscitation. Therefore, oxygen becomes the essential element to free hydrogen and raise the energy level of the water molecules for us as the life entity of water. This is the reason why oxygen inhalation is the most effective method to activate the life energy for an emergency resuscitation of consciousness.

3-38. Excessive oxygen domination makes active oxygen

We have the destiny that oxygen is the element which allows us to live and at the same time makes us to die. The peroxide-oxidized solution of water molecules with two oxygen atoms for two hydrogen atoms is called hydrogen peroxide. In hydrogen peroxide, an oxygen

Chapter Three ☆ The Turning Point

atom is attached over water molecules, so water molecules have stronger oxygen domination toward hydrogen. This hydrogen peroxide is called active oxygen. This active oxygen greatly restricts hydrogen atoms and water molecules by preventing the activation of life energy. This becomes a major cause of illness and aging.

The next important body domination structure in bio-molecular structure, other than water molecules, is organic materials such as sugars, starch, glucose, and cellulose. And the fundamental molecular structure of organic materials is dominated by a covalent bond or ionic bond with mainly oxygen, as the center with the higher atomic number, followed by hydrogen and carbon, forming a six-membered ring structure like a tortoise shell. Oxygen frees the ground energy in the molecular level of organic materials, and makes the energy level increase or decrease, and presides over the body activity. So, oxygen is the essential and important element required to keep our body alive.

Since water is formed by relativity with hydrogen and oxygen, oxygen is the most effective and essential element rather than nitrogen and carbon. And in order to have a healthy and long life, we should release the oxygen dominating structure by oxygen, effectively, and live our life not making excessive oxygen dominating structure by exhausted ion. Moreover, in order for hydrogen to be set free from the active oxygen, active hydrogen is an effective element as well. When we take natural water containing rich active hydrogen, we can expect a very good effect for our body. So in my opinion, in the future, active hydrogen water will become the mainstream for health.

3-39. Ancient lives succeeded in obtaining oxygen

Even in the field of science or history, there is no guaranteed fact or truth. Under the concept of time axis, which human beings created, everything exists in a hypothesis based on supposition, so I would like to verify, according to the PARAREVO theory, the hypothesis of "giant impact" as follows.

The earth was hit by Mars called the "giant impact," and a part of the earth broke off and became the moon. Because of the gravitational effect of the moon which happened at that time, water from Mars was scattered in the universe as ice clusters, and by the gravitation of the earth, ice clusters gradually moved and water appeared on the earth. And because of the relative original power of trinity, between the crystal deformation, the sun, and the moon, the role and the responsibility of Mars in the solar system carried over to the earth, and gradually hydrogen, oxygen and nitrogen covered the surface and formed the atmosphere, preparing the environment for "the prison star."

The original life entity, bacteria and virus, was born from an anoxic condition, and at that time, oxygen was only a life-threatening poisonous gas for ancient life entity. However, a type of bacteria appeared to boldly challenge oxygen at the risk of its own life and eventually succeeded in taking oxygen into the body. It was cyan bacteria. This was the era which accomplished life evolution rapidly in the process of evolutionary history. Cyan bacteria succeeded in creating a burst of energy beyond comparison by taking oxygen into the body, and making water molecules and organic molecules free. For this system, the earth organisms began to walk the path of evolution, rapidly.

Of course, not only at the molecular level, but also the energy conversion in the macro level came to be achieved by oxygen. Glycolysis and respiration of organic substances have been working with this mechanism by oxygen. The terrestrial life composes ATP (adenosine troposphere) from ADP (adenosine diphosphate) by using energy, which was obtained by nutrients from a composition of light and oxygen, and stores the energy in the molecules. When our body needs energy for movements, synthesis of body substances, temperature maintenance, bio-power generation, and bioluminescent, body organisms use the energy generated by converting ATP to ADP, and also decomposing high-energy phosphate bonds.

The molecular structure of water, which is essential for biological activity, and also in the molecular structure of organic substances, by releasing the organic domination and making each molecules field free, provided the system to raise the whole energy level of water molecules and organic molecules by the relative original power with oxygen.

3-40. Mechanism of respiration and oxidation

As indicated by the following formula, respiration is $C6H12O6 + 6O2 \rightarrow 6O2 + 6H2O$. This is the method by which oxygen is added to glucose and is converted to carbon dioxide and water. Energy is radiated by releasing the oxygen dominating structure by oxygen. So, the reason we can lose weight is because fat is reduced by aerobic exercise and converted into energy. However, to release the oxygen dominating structure by oxygen and convert it into energy means to destroy the molecular structure at the same time. This phenomenon is called oxidation.

To destroy the molecular structure by oxidation phenomenon means that the thing itself is disintegrated. The typical oxidation phenomenon is burning the material. The material burns when there is more calorific value than its ignition point of oxygen and the material, and when the material is burned, it is destroyed and eventually becomes ash.

Our body also lives by oxygen, and becomes ill by active oxygen, then ages and dies. However, active oxygen does not play only a bad role. When active oxygen and sodium ions react, ion channels of sodium are open and tiny electric current, the nerve transmitter substance, flows and transmits to the brain which perceived it as an itch. When active oxygen and calcium ion react, ion channels of calcium are open and transmitted to the brain as pain. So, since we perceive itch and pain by the relative original power of active oxygen and mineral ions, active oxygen is an essential substance.

Also for the neurotransmitter, minerals are essential substances. In this way, oxidation has the system that diffuses energy to the direction of material destruction in the life activity based on the increase of entropy, and the material itself will disappear, based on the decrease of entropy.

Eventually, the body will be reduced to ashes and bones, which will, in time, also disappear. Therefore, it is important to avoid excessive exercise, and reduce oxidation by active oxygen, and preserve oxygen in the body. "The secret of long life is a long breath," so the breathing method is important in order to release the oxygen

Chapter Three ☆ The Turning Point

dominating structure.

At the current biochemistry level, the prospect in phenomenon of the first and the last, and theoretical and empirical formulas based on the theoretical system exist, but that does not match the fact. This is because natural science is based on hypotheses such as theory and speculation; but nothing has been clarified regarding the process.

The DNA dominating structure is the macro dominating structure for the body, and the micro dominating structure is "the oxygen dominating structure" in the water and organic substances, which is more direct and primitive. In the treatment of carotid artery, when applying pressure on the carotid artery, blocking oxygen to the brain, it is possible to separate the spiritual consciousness entity from the body temporarily, and cause altered states of consciousness.

Using the breathing method of Indian Kundalini yoga, it is possible to experience a phenomenon by hyperventilating and cause hypoxic-ischemic encephalopathy temporally by reducing oxygen to the brain. However, if you perform this method out of mere curiosity, it can be very dangerous and cause severe spiritual disorders and schizophrenia, and may lead to definitive spiritual disabilities. When you block oxygen completely, the spiritual consciousness entity will secede from the body and you die.

3-41. The energy wave of the moon is the border between the spiritual world and this world

The earth star is the only water planet in the solar system, and although the life entity on the earth star is not able to survive without water, it is also restricted by the gravitational force of the atmosphere caused by water. By the water dominating structure which is the core of the physical dominating structure, the spiritual consciousness entity exists as complex life entity directed to inconvenience. We have been forced to exist by the fated system of the prison star according to the "principle of dependence and domination," and, even though we are dominated by the core of the oxygen dominating structure, we are not able to survive without oxygen.

The energy wave level of the moon is in a higher spiritual dimension than the wave level of the earth star, so it is possible to release the oxygen dominating structure by the energy of the higher dimension by transcending at the element level. The energy wave of the moon is the most familiar presence, which directs the integration of the body and the soul. Air, water, and food for life activities of the body on the earth star are only the relative original power of the substantial world in between the elements. However, relative particle and energy waves, flowing brilliantly from the moon, are the microscopic world which creates the relative original power in the ultra-relative particles dimension, such as elementary particles and top quark.

It is proven that the aura of the moon is much smaller than the aura of the earth star, and belongs in the higher dimensional energy level. Our aura is determined by our personality and spirituality dimension. And the dimension of the aura for fixed stars and planets is also determined by their spiritual dimension of the spiritual consciousness entity.

Chapter Three ☆ The Turning Point

The energy wave of the moon is located on the border line between the spiritual world and the substantial world, and relates to the earth star extremely closely. It functions as fusion to the body, so it will be possible to become the phenomenon like atomic conversion of the body, and make or cure illness of the body.

3-42. Roles and responsibilities of the moon toward the earth

All terrestrial life inhabiting *the prison planet* have common biological activities even though they have different shapes and forms, which are based on the common desire consciousnesses. The purpose is to complete the dietary desire consciousness and the sexual desire consciousness. Even though we acknowledge our death, we are continuing the way of life to live for living for the physical world benefits for an immediate profit, and our lifetime will end that way.

Since the moon existed before the birth of terrestrial life, we either do not pay much attention about the moon because it is always there, or we are dominated by the physical world benefits and think that the moon has no benefit. In any case, we have no interest or no intention to think about the presence of the moon. It seems that human beings have no interest at all if there are no economic benefits for us.

If the sun and the moon have no relation to terrestrial life, they would not have such a sense of presence among the infinite number of stars. For the earth star, based on the "rule of entropy relativity," the sun and the moon are directing the antipodes, the yin (negative) and the yang (positive). From the earth, the apparent size of the sun and the moon are exactly the same. If they have no role and responsibility toward the earth, it would not seem such a phenomenon. If the moon and the sun exist without any role or responsibility for the earth, their existence would lose significance and meaning. In order to take advantage of the energy wave from the moon, we must raise the spiritual dimension of our spirit.

Some astronomers and natural scientists are saying that "the earth star is the only planet in the solar system which has intelligent life." However, based on the spiritual dimension of the earth level with the physical visual range, it is impossible for them to know what the moon really is. With the knowledge level of scientists and human beings at the spiritual consciousness entity of lower spiritual dimension, it is absolutely impossible, and difficult to understand, what is the role and responsibility of the moon toward the earth star.

Even though the moon exists as an undeniable fact, it is the same as nothing if we are not conscious of it. When we look around, there are many things existing, but the existences themselves are denied if we are not aware of them. However, the moment we awaken to the existence of something, we are able to share the existence purpose and the value of the thing by the relative original power.

In order to create the relative original power by correlating it with the relative wave of the energy wave of the moon, we must each take part in the individuality as the integration unity with SHINSEI as the common denominator, and direct the spiritual relativity to the "principle of dimensional integration" and make a commitment to it. In doing so, we should derive the relative original

Chapter Three ☆ The Turning Point

power by the integrative relative energy (IRE) with logos, which connect to the spiritual entity living in the moon, and the method of breathing based on the SHINSEI integration consciousness, as the trinity. When we do this, we should take caution and do not disturb the inhabitants of the moon.

The energy wave of the moon is not able to be relative with the seven chakras. It requires a different chakra to connect and create the relative original power, universally, by IRE. It will be possible to induce the spiritual energy of the moon, selectively and intentionally, to ill organs and heal the illnesses. If medical science develops a way to use the energy wave of the moon efficiently, it will be able to achieve rapid progress and build the system without any expense and task for the patient.

In order to establish the spiritual world of the moon, we should learn how to create the relative original power by transcending the earth dimension based on the PARAREVO way of life, and direct the consciousness to the moon and achieve dimensional integration, and connect the relative wave with the energy wave of the moon actively.

We can release the oxygen dominating structure of water molecules in the body with the spiritual energy wave of the moon by Kunbahaka, the holy suppression of respiration, and release the spiritual consciousness entity from the physical domination at the microscopic dimension, not the genetic domination. By IRE, at the primitive microscopic dimension rather than the gene control, we should release the soul, the spiritual consciousness entity, and chakras from the physical domination and lighten the entire weight to prepare for the spiritual life. So, we should create the relative original power based on the moon and the spirit and mind, and open the emotional passage to the higher level with love and joy, then achieve Self-completion with SHINSEI integrated world as an individual art.

3-43. Solar energy waves affect the mind

The energy wave of the moon is an essential presence to accomplish the creation and the regeneration in the whole creator world, and has a great influence on the physical wave. The energy wave of the sun has a great influence on our mental wave and is an essential presence in order to form mental harmony and peace.

The energy wave of the full moon is effective for promoting secretion of dopamine and adrenaline, and stimulating the sympathetic nervous system, raising brain waves to beta waves and game waves, uplifting the spirits, activating the sexual desire consciousness and physical energy. In reverse, the energy wave of the sun promotes secretion of the brain hormones, endorphins, serotonin and noradrenaline, and stimulates the parasympathetic nervous system, levels brain waves to alpha waves, theta waves, and delta waves.

The three places with the highest rate of suicide in Japan are Akita, Aomori and Iwate, the three northeastern prefectures. In Europe, Norway and Sweden in Scandinavia are known as high rate of suicide places. The background and history in those Scandinavian countries bringing them to be known as the welfare states are because of the elderly suicides causing serious social problems.

Chapter Three ☆ The Turning Point

The daylight hours of the sun and mental motivation have a very close relationship. By absorbing the energy wave of the sun consciously, it will be possible to stabilize the mind and induce brain waves to sleeping mode and prevent depression and sleep disorder. Many people in the South Seas area, such as Fiji, Tahiti, and the Solomon Islands, spend most of the day napping, and it is proven that the numbers of depression and suicides are extremely low in these southern countries. The main causes of suicide are psychiatric disorders such as depression, eating disorders, and schizophrenia, and those are always accompanied with sleep disorders. The daylight hours of the sun supply not only vitamin D but also have a big influence mentally, so people who cannot sleep because of depression should take the energy from the sun, actively.

As you know, plant respiration occurs when pigments, such as chlorophyll and flavonoids, absorb the light and decompose water by photosynthesis and make hydrogen and oxygen, and at the same time it composes ATP (adenosine triphosphate) from ADP (adenosine diphosphate) which is the power of the physical life entity and the energy source. Simultaneously, it produces organic compounds as carbohydrates such as glucose, starch, and cellulose. In the formula, photosynthesis looks like the opposite reaction to respiration, but in fact, it is not a reversible reaction since it occurs in the intracellular and extracellular. This formula shows only the beginning and the end, but the process is very complex and still unclear. As I mentioned above, there is the complex and mysterious field of chemistry (inorganic chemistry) and biochemistry (organic chemistry), and even supposition or establishing a hypothesis is not possible.

So, I tried to explain it, by verifying the existing purpose and value of the sun according to actual phenomenon. Let's assume this as a magic of the sun. It is magic to generate oxygen and other totally different things such as flavonoids as multi-carotene, carotenoid, alpha-carotene, beta-carotene, zeaxanthin, lutein and lycopene using pigments in the cell as light catalyst. Thus, the presence of the sun is essential for life entity on the earth star.

The sun is not only providing light and heat, but it provides us with various energy waves, more than the moon. Especially, the energy wave of the sun has a big influence in the pineal gland in the brainstem, the pituitary gland, the thalamus, and the hypothalamus. The sun energy is entering from a special chakra, which is not one of the seven chakras commonly known, and has a huge effect for healing of mental disorders. When we lack the energy of the sun, it causes a metabolic shortage because it becomes difficult to generate hormones, such as endorphins and serotonin. This causes the reversal phenomena of day and night, and becomes the reason for the onset of mental disorders, social withdrawal, personality disorders, and action disorders, such as schizophrenia, depression, and insomnia.

3-44. Solar energy waves are feminine "negative" nature

Another important function for the sun energy is to release worldly desires existing in the brain, in where greed in the instinctive remaining consciousnesses, by the genetic domination of human beings, is accumulated.

Chapter Three ☆ The Turning Point

When we learn to create the energy wave of the sun and the relative original power by IRE (integrative relative energy) from a chakra, and master how to sublimate and purify the evil spirit, we will no longer worry about unnecessary desire, delusion, illusion, anxiety, and fear, so we will not connect the relative wave with the spiritual presence in poor spiritual dimension. As a result, our body clock will start functioning properly and the health and fortunes will improve. Spiritual presences, such as evil spirits, existing in the lower spiritual dimension of the "Astral plane," the "ghost world," are active at night to avoid the energy wave of the sun. Many criminal activities taking place at night are based on the external factor by the relative original power, and crimes and incidents occurring during the daytime are mostly based on the internal factor by the relative original power.

Since our exercise in consciousness and behavior based on the motivation are determined by the relative wave in the spiritual dimension and the "rule of the relative original power," we must connect the relative wave with the sun, which gives light and heart to good-natured or wicked people, rich or poor, unconditionally and equally, without asking for anything in return. And in doing so, we are directed to the intention of the sun according to the "principle of dimensional integration," and will be able to act based on great virtues of unselfishness with Self-sacrifice by free love.

The sun, which contains all philosophies, is an inevitable presence for Self-Enlightenment and spiritual evolution. However, since we are used to the presence of the sun from our birth, human beings have no real appreciation or joy toward the sun, and spend our life just taking care of the immediate profits. We only make use of the sun for the solar energy, heat, light and power generation, which are the range of visual light in the substantial dimension of the "Ether plane."

Based on the rule of entropy, women and the sun are the relative subjectivity, and men and the moon are the relative objectivity, so that the sun is feminine "negative" nature, and the moon is male "positive" nature. In order to connect the relative wave with the spiritual presence of the feminine negative nature existing in the sun, and link the spiritual line, we should manifest the "SHINSEI integration consciousness," integrate the logos and the method of breathing to the trinity, and lead the spiritual energy wave of the sun by IRE to a different chakra, other than the seven major chakras, and guide to Self-Enlightenment and spiritual evolution.

3-45. True Self-discovery is to discover SHINSEI

The purpose of life is Self-discovery, and Self-discovery is the means to find individuality. Finding individuality is discovering the one thing you really love and enjoy, the thing to which you can passionately devote your life. Discovering the thing you really live for means to find the best relative partner in whom you never lose interest. This partner should be the precious presence, and the essential presence to you.

Finding true presence, the *relative best partner,* who will accept your existence unconditionally and totally, and who is the one inevitable existence for you, is to find SHINSEI, which is the source of power that makes it possible for the soul, the spiritual consciousness entity, to exist forever, and to sustain generation and

Chapter Three ☆ The Turning Point

development. The priority purpose of life is to meet with true, loyal existence, SHINSEI, which is the relative subjectivity of true-life entity, based on the rule of entropy, and to discover the existence of SHINSEI, and identify yourself with it. SHINSEI does not exist somewhere in the universe, but exists inside of yourself between the first and second chakras.

Although the physical eyes are facing outside, the eyes of the spiritual consciousness entity are always facing inside, so we should separate our own "body mind" and direct consciousness to our "soul mind" according to the "principle of dimensional integration by internal separation" based on the rule of "spirit is subjective and body is objective," and recognize deeply that we are captive on the prison star with the wrongdoer consciousness and the principle of Self-responsibility, and should raise the spiritual dimension by the way of life of PARAREVO, which accepts as they are, unconditionally and totally with humility and modesty.

We should not select a momentary life which invites Self-destruction, falling into Self-hatred and Self-denial with Self-inflicted activities by unpleasant feelings and have victim consciousness, shifting responsibility to others, which directs responsibility consciousness to the outside, such as that person is bad or this person is a problem or this person has responsibility, etc., according to the "principle of dimensional domination by external separation," based on the rule of "body is subjective and spirit is objective."

Spiritual evolution on the earth star, the prison planet, is *finding SHINSEI as your own internal subjective presence and shifting the value of "body is subjective and spirit is objective," to the value of "spirit is subjective and body is objective,"* and to make the effort to clean your own SHINSEI, which is a divine shinning ball, like the Sun, but has gotten dirty by your *"body mind."*

By finding SHINSEI which exists eternally as the subject of love and guarantees freedom based on the PARAREVO theory, we are able to live a way of life which allows us to achieve Self-completion of the existing purpose and the existing value on the earth star.

Our SHINSEI and the universe are *the same root and the same spirit,* and when our body dies, our spiritual consciousness entity will return into our SHINSEI. The universe we see with our eyes is the physical universe and is far from us, however, the spiritual universe we will go to after we die is SHINSEI which exists as it is, deep inside us, and thus it is so close to us.

3-46. Excessive desire consciousness and the brain dominating structure

The core of the "instinctive survival consciousnesses," which are the common desire consciousnesses for the terrestrial life, have been inherited as worldly desires by memories of DNA of the brain by the "rule of the genetic chain." Since SHINSEI is the presence which can transcend the physical body and integrate the spiritual consciousness entity, it is important to aim to release the body domination during the resuscitation period.

In order to do so, we should release all domination desires which are the excessive physical world benefits, not only sexual desire, but also status desire, reputation desire, and acquisition competition for the evaluation of others. We should also release the material desire

Chapter Three ☆ The Turning Point

and the excessive appetite created by the economic supremacy doctrine and direct to the spiritual world benefits.

Since the knowledge of human beings is equal to nothing compared with the wisdom of the universe, we should clarify the usage of love and wisdom, and minimize the desire for the physical world benefits. It will be important work to direct the information of the genetic consciousness in the brain to a higher level, and evolve it by aiming for the genetic recombination.

As an example, when the consciousness is dominated by excessive material desire based on the rule of "body is subjective and spirit is objective," the tumor suppressor gene, the "soul mind," which directs the function of a normal cell is destroyed and the integration structure is converted to the domination structure by the cancer cell, the "body mind," and the cell becomes cancerous. If we can reverse this phenomenon based on the rule of entropy relativity according to "spirit is subjective and body is objective," it will be possible to make the genetic recombination by directing the genetic information in the brain to a higher level. A gene is composed of four molecules: adenine, cytosine, guanine, and thymine, and forms a molecular structure, a mononucleotides, which is the smallest genetic unit. The genetic codes, which are the structural arrangement of the genes, are formed by combination and arrangement of those four genes.

If we can convert the genetic combination and arrangement by the higher dimensional energy wave, treatments of schizophrenia, mental illness, depression and panic disorder would be possible, theoretically, by improving the integration and the domination nature of mind and body. This means that it will be possible to access a part of the body and a part of the genetic code by the creation power of IRE, which integrates the Trinity of SHINSEI integration consciousness, respiration, and logos from the chakras. By doing this, it becomes possible to transcend the body domination, and realize the consciousness transformation, which is a trance personality, and will enable us to improve mental disorders.

Furthermore, we will be able to sense the presence of SHINSEI by the power of IRE, beyond the theory or logic, unconditionally.

3-47. The 5 conditions for spiritual evolution

Life on the earth star has evolved from the bacteria of the prime life entity, through cyanobacteria, to various vertebrates, and then to human beings. That was caused by the experiences and adaptations to the different environmental changes. And, even though human beings are reigning at the top of the food chain, we are now facing an important era, according to the Buddhism term, Mappo, meaning the closing days of this world. So we must achieve a new spiritual evolution for this period of decline.

In the 21st century, we are finally achieving the evolution, which is not the evolution we experienced in the past, but the one in which we could reach the dimension of free spiritual life entity. Then it might be possible for us to join the universal life entity, like butterflies which undress the body and hatch beautifully from chrysalises. We human beings have come to the point to complete the spiritual evolution up to the universal dimension by securing the principle of Self-responsibility by accepting everything as it is, unconditionally and totally, in order to guarantee the rule of

Chapter Three ☆ The Turning Point

freedom.

So, the best way to achieve Self-Enlightenment and spiritual evolution is explained like this:

Making SHINSEI the common denominator in the slight fluctuation of imperfection between the two intentions, "soul mind," which is spiritual consciousness entity directing to the spiritual world benefits, and "body mind," which is the body directing to the physical world benefits, the important task and responsibility for each of us is how to direct the criterion of "soul mind," the relative subjectivity, to the higher level according to the "principle of dimensional integration" by internal separation, and achieve Self-Enlightenment and spiritual evolution based on SHINSEI integration consciousness."

First, in order to graduate from the prison star, *it is important to connect the relative wave with the person who is in a higher spiritual level of the higher spiritual dimension, and achieve the creation of joy with motivation of love by the relative original power based on the spirit and mind.* For that, we must first live a life of PARAREVO of SHINSEI unity, which directs to SHINSEI integrated life entity while verifying the presence of SHINSEI, by discovering our true self and achieving Self-completion.

Second, in order to connect the relativity with the spiritual dimension of the higher dimension, we should accomplish the Self-completion of true personality formation.

Third, in order to connect the relative wave with the spiritual dimension in the higher dimension, we should free the chakras, the spiritual antenna, and improve the spiritual ability of Chakras.

Fourth, after we establish the true personality formation and free the chakras, we must look for the spiritual entity in the higher dimension which would connect us with the relative wave and achieve the role and responsibility to graduate from the earth star, create the relative original power of the higher dimension, and achieve Self-completion of the true spiritual formation by exercising the consciousness of love and behave with joy as motivation.

Fifth, putting together all conditions, we should unify as the Trinity of SHINSEI integration consciousness, Chakras, and the spiritual wave of the spiritual entity in the higher dimension, create the relative original power, invoke the subjective consciousness of love, and achieve Self-completion of Self-Enlightenment and spiritual evolution by behaving with the creation of joy, as motivation, to all objects.

Those are the conditions required to graduate from the earth star, as the prison planet, and in order to achieve spiritual evolution, we must apply Self-effort, take Self-responsibility and make Self-completion.

3-48. The blind spot of the Mobius loop of "vertical love" and the core of ONSHU

In order to graduate from the earth star, the prison planet, we have to achieve spiritual evolution to the spiritual dimensional level which allows us to graduate. At the minimum, *we should not create any sorrow and ONSHU toward anything in this world or leave them in ourselves.*

The core of ONSHU in each of us, which will be the blind spot of the Mobius loop of love, is formed by the three layer structure of the

Chapter Three ☆ The Turning Point

triangle system of SHINSEI, which is the central presence, the soul ("soul mind") which is the intention of the spiritual consciousness entity, and the body ("body mind") which is the desire of the physical body.

Based on the rule of entropy relativity, the spiritual consciousness entity directs to form the core of love according to the rule of "spirit is subjective and body is objective," and the body directs to form the core of ONSHU according to the rule of "body is subjective and spirit is objective." Since ONSHU does not exist in a far distance but exists very close to us, the true and the closest ONSHU in each of us is the presence of the physical body, and the next closest presence of ONSHU is the relationship between parent and child.

The vertical relationship of parent and child is the most important connection to form the love of the spiritual consciousness entity and the core of ONSHU. It is significant because it determines, unconsciously, whether it directs to Self-Enlightenment and spiritual evolution according to the "principle of dimensional integration" of love, or whether it directs to the poor personality destruction and the spiritual degeneration according to the "principle of dimensional domination" of ONSHU. This is because, the relationship between parent and child shoulders the biggest assignment in the personality formation history, gives a great influence on Self-Enlightenment and spiritual evolution, and will become the blind spot of the Mobius loop of love, since it tends to achieve Self-formation of the core of love and ONSHU.

The Mobius loop of love is *the mechanism to create eternal sustainable energy as the SHINSEI integration consciousness entity, and is the universal system which makes it possible to sustain generation and development, and is always directing to a higher spiritual dimension according to the "principle of dimensional integration" by the fluctuation of the opposite relative original power derived from the slight fluctuation of imperfection by the pair system of SHINSEI and the spiritual consciousness entity.* When the "body mind" invokes, the "soul mind" also invokes to surpass the "body mind" based on the "rule of entropy relativity." The universal life entity that combines this mechanism and the system is called *"SHINSEI integrated life entity" based on the integration type of the Mobius loop.*

The blind spot of the Mobius loop of "vertical love" is formed in the closest relationship of parent and child, and the existence of this relationship is natural, since birth, just like the existence of the sun, the moon and air. So, because of the closeness, it is easy to create the dark shadows of ONSHU unconsciously. This dark shadow makes it easy to lose track of the true existing purpose and the existing value of the relationship of parent and child, and it is the result of adding more ONSHU on top of the core of ONSHU, up to the past life in the personality formation.

The primary purpose of the existence of parent and child is to release the core of ONSHU connoted in them. The core of ONSHU is the cause, the problem, and the assignment enclosed in their souls. Even though they are the closest existence physically, spiritually they are far apart, so they must understand that they are chosen as parent and child to release their ONSHU. In order to do so, they must try to establish their relationship, taking care of each other with the deepest true love, more than they do to anybody else.

However, in the non-PARAREVO world, generally speaking,

Chapter Three ☆ The Turning Point

parent-child relationships allow, as normal, violence and verbal abuse without remorse toward each other, which are absolutely forbidden toward others, based on the idea that it is OK because they are parent and child.

The essential human dignity, however, should be the same whether they are parent and child, married couples, or someone else. Since the parent-child relationship is the important one to shoulder the role and the responsibility to release the core of ONSHU from the past, they have to show their respect to each other with dignity and delicacy, more than others. Even though we can make objective criticism and evaluation to others, the parent-child relationship is too natural and close, so we can easy fall into an incomprehensible blind spot and can't see our ONSHU because we become short-sighted in ONSHU itself. Because of ignorance, parent and child are both hurting their soul, spiritual consciousness entity, intensely, and become poor and ugly personalities. We are repeating this unwise relationship throughout our history.

In the PARAREVO world, the parent-child relationship understands clearly that their relationship has been selected for and by each other for the purpose of spiritual evolution, according to the equation that *releasing your own ONSHU by loving ONSHU,* so there is the concept that *it can't be acceptable just because we are parent and child* as the basic philosophy. The base of love is parent-child relationship, so we must consider the importance of this relations more than other relations, so we should build the relationship our best with respecting each other's dignity, love each other deeply, understand and take care of each other well, and establish the core of love strongly.

The distance and the size of the blind spot of ONSHU will make a big difference whether the parent side or the child side has relative subjectivity between their relations. When the parent side has the relative subjectivity, it goes back one generation in the history of evolution by the time axis domination, so that the blind spot with SHINSEI becomes bigger, and it would be extremely difficult for Self-Enlightenment and spiritual evolution. When the relative subjectivity is under the child's side, it follows the history of evolution, so that the blind spot with SHINSEI becomes smaller, and will be directed to Self-Enlightenment and spiritual evolution.

In Japan, there in an old saying that *be guided by your children when you are old.* But if we think that the parent is the cause and the child is the effect, then it would happen that parents dominate children and impose their thoughts and their sense of values such as study, do this, do that, and by making excessive demands as privatization. It will increase the blind spot of the Mobius loop. As a result, it would amplify the distortion of the spherical theory and the relationship of ONSHU, and they will be directed to poor personality formation by falling into unpleasant feelings toward each other.

We must recognize that the soul of the child is the cause and the gene of the parent is the effect to be chosen, according to the "rule of reincarnation" based on the "rule of causality" of the spiritual consciousness entity. Parents, as the position of physical effect, face to the soul of child, as the position of spiritual cause, sincerely, serve submissively and follow the child's true nature with modesty and humility, then, they will release the blind spot of the Mobius loop and it will be possible to achieve ideal personality formation of

Chapter Three ☆ The Turning Point

love of the sphere integration.

The essential period to form the most important "true core," the core of love and ONSHU, created by the blind spot of the Mobius loop of vertical love, starts at the moment of descent of the soul of a child to a mother's womb by impregnation. So, during the time which the fetus is in the womb, united with a mother, in its sanctuary for spiritual evolution and physical evolution, and the closest time of the blind spot of the Mobius loop, a mother has to do her best to treat her fetus well and love it deeply with her heart in order to complete the spiritual improvement and the physical improvement according to the "rule of change by birth and re-birth" based on the PARAREVO theory.

The most ugly and inferior things of human beings are Self-hatred and Self-denial. Those are the worst core of ONSHU and the root of all evil. So how would we form Self-hatred and Self-denial in ourselves, by ourselves?

Although the spiritual consciousness entity had made Self-determination of the genes and the parents under free intention, in order to achieve spiritual evolution, if they are the poor genes and the parents contrary to the expectations, feeling of hatred and denial of the same amount of the expectations will be formed, unconsciously, and become Self-hatred and Self-denial and enclosed inside of themselves, according to the "rule of adaptation." Especially, feelings of hatred and denial in the womb, which is the sanctuary of the spiritual evolution and the physical evolution, will form the true core of the most fundamental ONSHU.

Thus, the fundamental cause for Self-hatred and Self-denial are the feelings of disillusionment, disgust, and hatred toward the parents and the genes of the parents, which are adapted unconsciously. There are many ways to reach Self-hatred and Self-denial. Mentally, it can be personality and nature, and physically it can be face, shape or appearance, and smart or foolish for ability. There can be considerable factors and incentives.

However, even though the physical body is inherited from the parents, the child's own spiritual consciousness entity, has decided the genes of the parents and the parents themselves based on the rule of freedom, so a child has to have the role and responsibility to overcome the assignment, shouldering the Self-responsibility to all things, by himself/herself. When parents and child both understand this, and they confirm and approve each other's role and responsibility by themselves, then unnecessary burdens will be released and meaningless ONSHU would not be formed at all.

According to the "rule of the universe," the "rule of freedom," all things are referred to Self-completion with Self-management and Self-determination by Self-responsibility. We must understand that the parents were selected under Self-determination by our own spiritual consciousness entity, and should make Self-completion to all assignments with Self-responsibility. If we fall into victim consciousness against the parents and ancestors who are no relation to our own soul, and follow the false theory of salvation by memorial services for ancestors, mistaking the means for the end, and shifting responsibility, this ONSHU will be adapted to yourself and restored as it is, and you will be directed to Self-hatred and Self-denial, unconsciously, fall into the negative spiral by Self-injurious behavior, piling mountains of unhappiness, and eventually heading to family breakdown and Self-destruction.

Therefore, if there is one reason we choose our parents, who are the birth-parents of the physical body, it is we who carry the past ONSHU in ourselves. So we must sincerely face to the genes of the parents, which are the past ONSHU of ourselves, and the fruit of the accumulation of the instinctive survival consciousnesses, then we should achieve Self-completion with Self-compassion, Self-affirmation and Self-acceptance. The best method to release ONSHU of the spiritual consciousness entity along the genetic domination, which has been inherited according to the "rule of the genetic chain" based on the "rule of physical causality," continuously, spiritual evolution together with the body throughout history, as the terrestrial life, is to release the blind spot of the Mobius loop of vertical love.

3-49. Love and ONSHU between parents and children have distorted the sexual differentiation

In the terrestrial life, there is a three layer structure of the triangle system with SHINSEI, the spiritual consciousness entity, and the body, and this creates a triangle relationship with SHINSEI, the "soul mind," and the "body mind," and raises various problems and complications. As a result of that, the core of ONSHU of the spiritual consciousness entity has been built by the two major desire consciousnesses by the instinctive survival consciousnesses, continuously.

Human beings have been tamed by the instinctive survival consciousnesses through 3.8 billion years, strengthened insatiable desires, and reined at the top of the food chain of terrestrial life. Human beings are the result of strengthening the physical dominating structure which continues to increase the quantity and quality of desires without any change, keeping the rule of "body is subjective and spirit is objective." Just like a drug patient who is addicted to pleasure and falls into drug dependence, human beings still keep looking for pleasures of the physical world benefits, by the desire of the body, and being directed to *the "principle of dependence and domination"* by the instinctive survival consciousnesses. Thus, we human beings are an extremely rare and foolish life entity in the universe, because we are satisfied with inconvenience.

Life entity in the higher spiritual dimension in the universe prepares the system which makes it possible to exist eternally, directing generation and development to a higher level by the mechanism of sphere integration which creates the sustainable relative original power by the pair system between SHINSEI and the spiritual consciousness entity in the slight fluctuation of imperfection.

Since the core of ONSHU is caused by the triangle relationship of the triangle system, ONSHU is Self-formed in various relationships such as, between the parents and child, among the married couples and their father-in-law and mother-in-law. For example, in the relationship between the parents and the boy, the relation of ONSHU is formed between a father and an elder son by the triangle relationship among the father, mother, and the elder son, and in the relationship between the parents and the girl, the relation of ONSHU is caused, inevitably, between a mother and an elder daughter unconsciously, by the triangle system among the father, mother, and the elder daughter. In general *it is forgiven because*

Chapter Three ☆ The Turning Point

of parent and child, so all things fall into unconscious unpleasant feelings, and the spiritual consciousness entity will dissipate little by little, and the core of ONSHU will be Self-formed, unconsciously.

The ideal personality formation of love is in the reverse relation, so that boys were born selecting the nature of man in order to evolve to a higher spiritual dimensional sexual differentiation by maternal love. Girls were born selecting the nature as woman in order to evolve to a higher spiritual dimensional sexual differentiation by paternal love. Completing this role and responsibility is the requirement to release the deviation between male nature and female nature, and ONSHU of love in the "negative" and the "positive" of parent and child. By directing to mental fusion by the rule of the "negative" and the "positive" of parent and child, it will be possible to become the integrated life entity with good balance.

Through the unfortunate history of human beings, the nature of ONSHU of love of parent and child has spoiled undifferentiated sexual desire consciousness, invited deviation and disgrace of sexuality, created lower human beings with undifferentiated sexual impulse, such as Kings, Shoguns, and foolish sovereigns produced to the world, building a vulgar history. This is the biggest cause and reason that we could not be directed to a higher spiritual dimension for our Self-Enlightenment and spiritual evolution. Since the blind spot of the Mobius loop of love in the "negative" and the "positive" of parent and child has formed undeveloped sexual differentiation against the spiritual evolution, also created lower human beings who have undifferentiated sexual impulse, and those people have taken over the politics, religions and economies, which were the sovereignty, with sexual desire as the center, society and history have been forced to form a poor world.

Lack and ignorance of the vertical love of paternity and maternity have directed to the "principle of dependence and domination," and the victim consciousness and the shifting of responsibility have become the cause of distortion in the personality formation, families, societies, and the nations. Thus, *the sexual differentiation and the spiritual evolution are the relative culture and civilization, so to be a higher dimension of the differentiation of sexuality will create a higher dimension of the spiritual dimension.*

3-50. The blind spot of the Mobius loop of "horizontal love" and the core of ONSHU of brothers and sisters

The next relationship to become the core of ONSHU toward love is between siblings. Both the relationship of parent-child and the relationship between siblings have a delicate tendency of deviation of love depending on the position of each.

For example, with each standing point, between eldest son and second son, or between eldest daughter and second daughter, love and ONSHU received from the parents are different. When the eldest brother is placed in the center of the family and raised with great care, there is a remarkable gap of love with his other brothers, and sometimes causes problems in inheritance and succession to the headship of the house.

First born son and daughter could dominate the love of the parents unconditionally, at the beginning, however, when younger brother and sister are born and need full support from the parents, the elder siblings feel that the amount of maternal love to them was

Chapter Three ☆ The Turning Point

reduced, so that they start taking confirmation action of love by bullying younger brother and sister because of jealousy and envy, or by being disobedient to the parents, according to the rule of the "exclusion theory by jealousy."

The common sense in the non-PAREVO world is that no matter how brothers and sisters curse each other with bitter words, or quarrel and fistfight, it is forgiven because they are brothers and sisters.

In many countries, if they behaved in such a way toward others, they would be charged as criminals in society. However, for example, in Japan, if parents punish the children and treat them cruelly, or siblings quarrel seriously with each other, it is the basic policy and attitude, that police or administration would not intervene at all, because it is a family matter. Especially today, the most serious problems in the deep dark part of society are elders dying alone and domestic violence by children, which is due to family breakdown.

Both the relationship of parent and child, and relationship of brothers and sisters would become unbelievably tenuous once being distorted, surfacing ugliness and poorness, would become unrepeatable, and will go to the spiritual world with additional ONSHU.

Since common sense in the PAREVO world would consider the core of ONSHU, based on the rule of the "exclusion theory by jealousy," brothers and sisters should face each other, and do their best with heart and mind with the concept that *it should not be forgiven only because they are brothers and sisters,* accept the existing purpose and dignity of each other, and consider it as one morality to build the relationship with delicacy. Of course, the best

Self-effort would be made toward brothers-in-law and sisters-in-law in order to build the relationship to treat each other well, love each other, and understand each other.

As you can see, common sense in the non-PARAREVO world and in the PARAREVO world are directed to totally opposite theoretical framework and values.

3-51. The blind spot of the Mobius loop of "horizontal love" and the core of ONSHU of husband and wife

Marital relationship is the "principle of dimensional integration" of "horizontal love," and is also directed to totally opposite vectors by the "rule of the universe" and the "rule of the earth." Since the earth is the prison star, the mechanisms and systems on the earth star are all penetrated by the "principle of dimensional domination." So, we cannot deny that the history of women, the relative subject, has been dominated by one-sided theoretical framework and values which were created by men, the relative object.

The blind spot of the Mobius loop of "horizontal love" is explained as follows. "Horizontal love" means the relationship of a married couple, and the Mobius loop means the mechanism and the system that create, eternally, universal *individual art based on free love* by the theory of sphere, which by making it possible to sustain generation and development by directing men's intention to women's intention. And the blind spot means that the distance and the wall of ONSHU with unpleasant feelings which are directed to inconvenience, by being restricted or dominated by the relative objectivity, men, and *hide the existence of SHINSEI, the central core*

Chapter Three ☆ The Turning Point

of love.

The distance and the size of the wall of the blind spot are quite different whether the subjectivity is on husband's side or wife's side, according to the relativity of the "negative" and the "positive." The existing purpose and the existing value of men and women are directed to the opposite principals based on the PARAREVO theory. Men connote the ideas of *power, domination, struggle and destruction* inside their consciousness, and women connote the ideas of *love, integration, harmony and creation* inside their consciousness. In order to direct Self-Enlightenment and spiritual evolution according to the "principle of dimensional integration," since women are the relative subjectivity and men are the relative objectivity, we should establish a family with the love of a married couple as the foundation by the pair system of women as subject, and then build societies, nations and the world.

However, the history of human beings has legalized the male dominating structure by undifferentiated sexual desire consciousness of men, reigned over many women with their power, and established the pyramidal organization and the social structure in the history, continuously. Men have legally created a great deal of ONSHU and sorrow, in history, toward women in the relationship of a married couple, by the "principle of dimensional domination." This is the primary reason to create The blind spot of the Mobius loop of "horizontal love." This is the biggest reason we could not reach the "Heaven" which is the world of a married couple.

On the earth star, men have created the convenient theoretical framework and the value, religiously, in order to dominate women legally. The Bible was written based on men's theory, such as "God formed man from the dust of the ground, and breathed into his nostrils, the breath of life; and man became a living soul. It was the birth of man and God called the man Adam. It was not good that the man should be alone, so God took one of Adam's ribs and created a woman and named her Eve."

That means woman was born from a man's body, and moreover, she was born from one of his ribs. I have never heard of a child who was born from the ribs or there was no such a fact confirmed. Also, I have never even heard or confirmed that a child was born from a man. After Eve was created from Adam's rib, children such as Cain, Abel and Seth were born through the womb of Eve. It is clear that the principle and fundamental rule of creation were distorted from the beginning and became a nonsensical fairy tale. Do you think God, who was created by religion as perfect and complete, would do such an inconsistent thing? If religions accept it, that fact is already meaningless, and unquestioning acceptance is nothing but fanaticism.

It is more natural that a woman was born first and later a man was born through the womb of the woman, but still I feel like something is wrong, like whether the chicken or the egg came first. Since the universe is obliged to exist by the rule of entropy relativity based on the fundamental "rule of the universe," neither men or women came first, however, strictly speaking, as long as the relative subjectivity is women, I would say that women slightly came first.

Therefore, the genetic information of mitochondria DNA is only preserved and inherited inside the cells of women. In the evolutionary process, starting from bacteria and virus, the primitive life entity,

Chapter Three ☆ The Turning Point

the progress of evolution improved as *the sexual differentiation of the spiritual consciousness* from the sex unified life entity such as a single amoeba, and transformed individually to the sex separation life entity of the physical "negative" and "positive," synchronically and simultaneously. Evolution has directed to the consciousness of the spiritual consciousness entity, based on the rule of "spirit is subjective and body is objective," and the physical body has evolved at the same time, and it has become the original and physical sex separation life entity of the "negative" and the "positive" as the archetypal form of male and female. It is neither the chicken nor the egg that came first. In the evolutionary process, the spiritual evolution, based on "spirit is subjective and body is objective," and the physical evolution, by the genetic recombination, has been done inside the womb of a female, synchronically and simultaneously, according to the "rule of change by birth and re-birth."

Since religion's theory clearly carry out the theory that man is the subject and woman is the object, in the root of the religious doctrine, so God is always "father," the masculine gender such as "Our Father in heaven" or "Father, Son and Holy Spirit." The presence of the feminine gender has been ignored and abused throughout history, and is the origin of religious discrimination against women. By the self-righteous logic of the male dominating structure, it is said that Eve became depraved and a symbol of adultery. All roots were shifted to women, and the pyramidal dominating structure has been built throughout history, continuously, in order to direct to the male legalized dominating structure.

As we can see in the Bible, there are many similar ancient stories in the world in which the woman is the one labeled as the sinner. For example, in "Kojiki" (Record of Ancient Matters), the oldest extant chronicle in Japan, when the male god named Izanagi and the female god named Izanami had the ceremony of intercourse for creating many nature gods, Izanami, the female god, invited the male god Izanagi, first. It was said that they created an imperfect creature. So they were told to do it all over again, and next, Izanagi, the male god, invited Izanami, and they created many perfect nature gods. This clearly suggests the male supremacy. Also, later, Izanami was the one sent to the land of the dead as a sinner.

Also, in Japan, men have never allowed women to enter the "sacred mountains," saying it was the line between a sacred place and unclean women. So, the dominating and egotistic theory of men has been carried through religiously.

The religious world should have formed a spiritual pillar; however, to accomplish the role to strengthen the domination in the substantial world, they made the delay of the spiritual evolution in the earth star. There we can see the desire and the attitude of men who have continued to refuse, stubbornly, the rise of women who played the role and responsibility of the integration of love and the evolution of the creation.

All times and places, all ages and countries, wherever we go, *there is the legalized male type dominating structure of men, by men and for men, and carry through the theory of power, domination, struggle and destruction.* Non- PARAREVO theory is constructed by the theoretical framework to accomplish the mission, roles and responsibility of the prison star. All mechanisms are directed to legalize the male type dominating structure, and are systematized from married couples to family, ethnic groups, nation, and the world.

Chapter Three ☆ The Turning Point

If the scriptures, the Bibles, and Buddhist literature were written about women as the subject, there would have been completely different logic, and prayer would have been as "Our Mother in heaven," or "in the name of Mother, child and the Holy Spirit."

The most foolish thinking by ignorance in human history is that the relationship of married couples has been directed to the opposite theory. In the non-PARAREVO world, although the theoretical subjectivity and objectivity are directed to the opposite, there is the blind spot of married couples.

Since the relationship is too close, we often hear that "it can be forgiven because they are a married couple" or "nobody will get involved in an argument between husband and wife." Those ideas have evolved, and the system of nonaggression and nonintervention has been justified under the men's sovereignty, and have historically built much sorrow and ONSHU of women. These are the biggest reasons that human beings still end the lifetime by continuing the common desire consciousness and the common ecology activities by being dominated by the physical thoughts, which are the same as other terrestrial life.

In the way of PARAREVO life, married couples clearly understand about the equation and the mechanism of the spiritual evolution and the physical evolution, so that they distinguish the role and the responsibility for the subjectivity of women and the objectivity of men, and would never be reversed by the "principle of dependence and domination."

Since the sanctuary for spiritual and physical evolution is inside the womb, it would be possible, by the "rule of change by birth and re-birth," to surpass the undifferentiated sexual desire consciousness of men by sacred sexual relations of a high level of sexual differentiation of women. Then the soul descends by birth from a higher spiritual dimension and achieves the spiritual quality improvement of according to the "rule of the relative original power" based on the spirit and mind, and by rearranging the last line of the genetic structural arrangement of women, accomplish the physical improvement as the soul of the child wishes, and the child is born to this world.

Since the equation and the mechanism of spiritual and physical evolution are given to women as the subjective authority, men are not able to graduate from the earth star, unless they re-birth to a higher soul by women according to the "rule of change by birth and re-birth." Even righteous men and saints are not able to be changed by birth without completing the marital love of SHINSEI unity in this world, and pass through the spiritual womb of a woman in the spiritual world. The PARAREVO world straightforwardly directs the married couple to connect with each other with tenderness, and have the concept as *"it is not forgiven because we are married couple."* And with the level of the higher dimension, open the feeling of love and joy in each other by the "pair system of love of SHINSEI unity." Those are the existing purpose and the existing value of life.

The major problem is that we as human beings do not understand that the consciousness form of men and the consciousness form of women are pointing in totally opposite directions. The consciousness form of men *is dominated by undifferentiated sexual desire consciousness, according to the instinctive survival consciousnesses, and always has a sexual fantasy toward women of their liking.* Men do not understand at all that women are fed up with men and that is their fundamental sorrow and ONSHU, since succumbing to the sexual desire domination of men, being thought of as sex objects unilaterally, and being used as sexual tools. This mental gap has become the major glitch and wall between married couples and between single men and women, and has brought up serious problems, challenges, and complications.

3-52. The 21st century is the creative era of spiritually wise women

With a glimpse of human history, it is quite easy to see that there have always been struggles by the male type dominating structure.

Up to the 20th century was the era of ideological struggles between capitalism based on liberalism, and communism based on socialism. Then, the first year into the 21st century, the September 11 attacks happened. Islamic fundamentalist terrorist groups, attacked the United States, and the era of religious struggles began. It all happened because of the male type dominating structure; however, because the "rule of the universe" is the priority, we have certainly achieved spiritual evolution by the "principle of dimensional integration."

In the 21st century, we should build a society of the female type integrated structure, globally, based on the PARAREVO theory, but not the society of the male type dominating structure based on the non-PARAREVO theory.

There are many backward countries where still openly legalized religious theories and laws of gender discrimination with the undifferentiated sexuality, such as adultery of men is accepted but women's is punished. Divorce by men is allowed but divorce by women is not allowed by the discriminating law against women. Also polygamy, which states that a man can determine the number of wives he takes depending on his economic ability, is a law.

In Japanese character, wife is written as woman in house or woman in room. Those are discriminate and dominant words, and they were made by men's theory of the "principle of dependence and domination," which means women have been dependent economically and men were the master of the house, so women were imprisoned and sent away to the back of the house and would not be able to go outside at all. Those words are derived from the ideas that describe women in Japan.

Up to the 20th century, the history of struggle and destruction by the male type dominating structure has been built, continuously, by men who do not have any connection to determine or right to inherit spiritual and physical evolution. The purpose of this structure has been directed to fulfill the function of the role and the responsibility for the prison star. Religious theories, such as the Bible, Buddhist literature, and scriptures, have been used for this purpose, so that they have switched "spiritual God" to "human God of the worldly benefits," and the true nature was hidden.

The distress and grief caused by the unfair discrimination against women have been spoken to God and Buddha, however, those women's appeals are not heard by God. The big problem is that originators of many religions have played a role as the guard of the prison star, so, to the contrary of saving the soul of women, they have legalized the men's theory and have built the pyramidal religious organizations. As a result, we have continued the history,

Chapter Three ☆ The Turning Point

such as in the Royal family in Japan, and even ordinary families, to protect the right of inheritance of men, but ignored the existence of women's rights.

However, as I mentioned before, women are the only ones who are able to accept the life entity to their womb and have the power of creation to produce the evolved new dimensional life entities by the "rule of change by birth and re-birth." The role and mission of men was to provide sperm by their sexual desire consciousness, and also to play a role and responsibility as the catalyst for egg cell division. This is shown by the fact that most of the genetic information by the "instinctive survival consciousnesses" have been internalized and the chain-preserved in women's mitochondria, which created the energy for the cell nucleus.

Since the spiritual dimension of the soul and the genetic information of the physical evolution are all given to women to determine and inherit the evolution by the universe, the casting vote for spiritual evolution and physical evolution are left to women's spiritual dimension, based on their sentimental world and personality dimension. In order to transcend the blind spot of the Mobius loop of "horizontal love," we should clarify the role and responsibility in the relationship between a married couple, and *convert the role and responsibility in this world, which has been building up until now largely from men to women.*

Unless we build the marital relationship in which the wife is the sexual subject and the husband is the sexual object, it will be impossible to surpass and transcend the blind spot of the Mobius loop of "horizontal love" according to the "rule of the universe," and it will be against the principle of dimensional integration of love.

So, without building up those relationships we would descend to the earth star, again and again, according to the "rule of reincarnation."

In the 21st century, spiritually wise women will receive a higher dimension of souls to their womb, which is the sanctuary for "changing by birth and re-birth," by "sacred impregnation relationship." And, I believe that the time will come when we will achieve the great spiritual evolution by the principle of responsibility of humans, and we will produce and increase rapidly, the life entities of the higher spiritual dimension to the earth star.

The way of the PARAREVO life will produce many spiritually wise women and they will banish polygamy and the value of patriarchal doctrine aiming for the domination of men over women. Spiritually wise women are the ones to build the love mechanism by the subject of women, create a spherical social system, and be able to live up to the way of PARAREVO life by the logic of "principle of independence and freedom."

So, women have to shoulder the responsibility to not depend on men, and make Self-effort for independence, to acquire real freedom suggested by the PARAREVO theory, and not become a housewife who only depends on her husband. Also in order to refuse to depend on the physical domination of the earth star and surpass and transcend the "instinctive survival consciousnesses," women must make the priority to achieve mental and economic independence.

Since women connote the conception structure to receive a spiritual soul, and have the spiritual structure and the physical structure to easily accept invisible power, and have strong inspiration and intuition, so when women achieve a social advancement, they will accomplish a big social contribution. Women have excellent

Chapter Three ☆ The Turning Point

brains, are filled with life force, and have highly receptive abilities, so except for lower physical capabilities, women are much superior to men in all respects. However, there has been no opportunity for women to manifest and display their real abilities, throughout history.

Up to the 20th century, in order to fulfill the function of the prison star, women's abilities have been suppressed and forced to the background by the male type dominating structure. However, in the 21st century, women should play a central role and responsibility in politics and economics, in the foreground of society. We must make a huge reformation from the paradigm of men's subject to women's subject, direct to the true spiritual evolution and aim for the world of co-existence, mutual prosperity, and symbiosis. Otherwise, we will invite the chain of unhappiness by the minus spiral, and could result in the world being destroyed by nuclear weapons of mass destruction.

3-53. Horizontal love of the Mobius loop and integration of sexuality

The male type dominating structure of the prison star will invite the result of the bias toward sexuality and destroy the personality balance of the "negative" and the "positive." Lower level human beings with poor spiritual dimension live in the non-PARAREVO theory and behave with the self-righteous theory of men, according to the theoretical framework and value of the prison star.

Women who live a way of PARAREVO life understand their role and responsibility which form the harmony and order to the higher level, so women, as the relative subjectivity, must integrate men, the relative objectivity, by love and direct them to a higher spiritual dimension, according to the "principle of dimensional integration" based on the "rule of entropy relativity."

The best personality for men and women with well balanced "negative" and "positive" is explained like this. Suppose that the percentage of "negative" and "positive" of the entire personality is 50 % and 50 %. A man, if he has 51% in the masculine "positive" nature and 49% in masculine "negative" nature in his personality in the slight fluctuation of imperfection between those natures, he is dimensionally dominated by the male side as lower consciousness of sexuality by deriving the relative original power of the "negative" and the "positive," so you could say that he will be the ideal man who is able to exercise the consciousness of a higher spiritual dimension and can behave by the motivation of goodness.

The masculine "positive" nature means that a man with a physical body has a strong tendency toward the male type soul, "masculine male nature." However, since the criterion of the "negative" and the "positive" in the soul are not limited merely to the man, because it is the aggregation of the complex spirituality formation history in the last life and other past lives when sometimes he was a man and sometimes he was a woman. Because of that, I will call them the "positive nature" and the "negative nature."

In the spiritual dimension of each soul, "soul mind" and "body mind" exist as opposites, unconditionally, in the slight fluctuation of imperfection, by the rule of entropy relativity, so, the invocation of the consciousness, motivation, and behavior, depending on the spiritual dimension of the "soul mind" and the "body mind," will be

Chapter Three ☆ The Turning Point

totally different.

Based on the rule of "spirit is subjective and body is objective," between the "positive nature" and the "negative nature" in the differential of sexual behavior, each person has, sometimes, male tendencies and sometimes female tendencies, so every person has a totally different nature and personality. Also the masculine "negative nature" is physically male but has a strong tendency toward the feminine nature contained in the soul.

However, if person has 90% of the masculine "positive nature" and 10% of the masculine "negative nature," he has a strong tendency of leaning toward the masculine "positive nature." This means that his past lives were predominantly male. This kind of person is biased to the nature and the personality in the male type sexual dominating structure, so he connotes undifferentiated sexual desire consciousness inside the spiritual consciousness entity, and has extremely dominant, combative, and destructive spirituality and the personality of a dictator. He is also very dominant toward women, and has a tendency to rein in the dominating classes. In fact, religious gurus, politicians, central government officials, and presidents and executives in companies, are expressing this tendency remarkably.

In the case of women, if a woman has 51 % of the female "negative nature" and 49 % of the female "positive nature," she will be a woman who has the least differential of sexual behavior and well-balanced personally. Also, women who have a tendency to lean toward the female "negative nature" are often the ordinary housewives who have a strong tendency of dependence toward men, and in rare cases, some put themselves in a sexually disgraced society such as sexual business to make money using their sexuality.

In order to accomplish Self-completion of the true personality formation, it is important that man and woman direct to the neutral and moderated personality formation together, by the pair system of SHINSEI unity, open the relative emotional path to each other with love and happiness, accept each individual mental entity as the individual art, and manifest as the sexual integrated art of the "negative" and the "positive." Married couples who live the PARAREVO life are in agreement with their existing purpose and existing value of life, share their life in common directing to Self-Enlightenment and spiritual evolution by loving, treating, understanding, and nurturing each other, so that it will be easier for them to complete the ideal love of the Mobius loop.

3-54. Pair system of love in the SHINSEI unity

The "rule of the universe" is forced to exist in the "negative" and the "positive" by the love pair system of SHINSEI unity, based on the PARAREVO theory.

The Bible was the historical book of slaughter and plunder of love, which has been proved by the "system of sorrow and ONSHU in the triangle relationship" and resulted in the male type sexual desire dominating structure. In fact, Jews who follow Judaism, and Arabs ethnic groups who follow Islam, have been fighting worldwide with struggles and slaughters to wash blood in blood, by the theory of "a god with the physical world benefits and the principal of right and wrong" based on monotheism.

In Christianity, because of the differences in the theoretical

Chapter Three ☆ The Turning Point

frameworks and values between Protestants and Catholics, in Northern Ireland, for instance, their conflicts are serious and deeply rooted, and they are still fighting with struggles and slaughters, holding sorrow and ONSHU. Moreover, the United States, which is the largest Christian nation, is still conducting wars and standing at the forefront in the world.

Religions still do not understand at all, whether they exist for struggles and slaughters, or whether they exist for improvement of the mental culture and peace. There are endless numbers of religions in the world, however, the fact is that each religion is exclusive, criticizes and evaluates other religions, and still struggle for the religious doctrines.

For the true proof, which is the fingerprint of history, the inheritance of the soul of sorrow and ONSHU, has been by the relative original power based on the women's spirit and mind, and physically, it has been inherited in mitochondria DNA by the major "negative" type in the genetic code of women's ovum, as the "instinctive remaining consciousnesses." In the 21st century, the triangle system of the pyramidal dominating structure of the prison star, which was established by the mechanism of the male type dominating structure, should be dismantled by spiritually wise women, based on the theory of PARAREVO, and release the sorrow and ONSHU held in history. Then it should be re-created to the pair system of the sphere type integrating structure and search for a new path for spiritual evolution reaching to the higher human being.

In order to complete the love pair system of SHINSEI unity in this world, we have to depend on women for the rule of "change by birth and re-birth." Even the saints are not able to achieve Self-completion of the personality formation of ideal love with the "negative" and the "positive" integration, by being alone in this world. They must release sorrow and ONSHU of a woman, and be changed by birth and re-birth by the woman. That is the rule of the universe. Since bachelor saints and righteous persons have not completed the role and responsibility toward the individual purpose, they would remain on the earth star until *regeneration of SHINSEI and the soul* is completed, according to the "rule of reincarnation" based on the "rule of spiritual causality."

Regeneration of SHINSEI and the soul means *to complete the pair system of SHINSEI and the soul, and achieve spiritual evolution to the SHINSEI integrated life entity, which is the sphere structure creating the sustainable energy eternally.*

3-55. History has been built with the love and ONSHU of women

Human history has been constructed by the male type dominating structure, superficially. However in reality, as written in the Bible, infertile women such as Sarah and Rachel had surpassed their ONSHU by love, and conceived by opening their closed womb by releasing their ONSHU by loving the ONSHU. So, as you can see, it has continued and evolved by the logic of love, integration, harmony and creation of women who have connected the chain of life with their love, as detailed in BOOK2. At the same time, in history, sorrow and ONSHU in the genetic chain have been also inherited by women, according to the reversed rule of entropy.

Chapter Three ☆ The Turning Point

The chain of fundamental love and creation in human history, and the chain of ONSHU and destruction have been left and determined in the spiritual dimension of women and the genetic code of ova. No matter how good the seed planted by a man, it will wither and die if the field of a woman is barren, or if it is an ordinary field, it will bear ordinary fruit. But, even though the seed is not a good one, if it is planted in a fertile field, it will grow well and many flowers will bloom and fruit will hang heavy on the branches.

It has a far more important and significant meaning of the criterion of the spiritual dimension of women and their ova than the criterion of the spiritual dimension of men and their sperm. Depending on the criterion of the "soul mind" and the "body mind" in the spiritual dimension of women, there will be a vast difference in the relative original power based on the spirit and mind in the conception relationship. For example, the dimension of the soul of a fetus by descent conception by impregnation relationship would be totally different between the women who are in the lower "Astral dimension" with a lewd mind, and the women who are in the higher "Causal dimension" with a noble mind. The mother who bore the saints and righteous persons, or the mother who bore the dictators and tyrants, such as Hitler, would have a huge difference in their spiritual dimensions.

Behind the saints was a mother who had a great sentimental world and personality dimension, but behind the dictators and tyrants, there was a mother who had poor sentimental world and personality dimension filled with ONSHU. There are excellent mothers in fine families, brilliant women in the good ethnic groups, and great and spiritually awakened women in the leading nation.

So, the journey of human history has been directed to evolutional history by women, as the relative subjectivity, based on the female type integrating structure, and achieved spiritual evolution gradually, over a long period of time.

In order to release the Mobius loop of "horizontal love," women and men should face each other with SHINSEI as the common denominator and the individuality as a molecule, based on the theory of PARAREVO, and direct to the "soul mind," according to the "principle of dimensional integration" by internal separation, build a love pair system of SHINSEI unity with loving, treating well, understanding, and nurturing each other. Also, they should share the existing purpose and the existing value of life to open the door to the "Heaven" for graduating from the earth star, and complete spiritual evolution to the "SHINSEI integrated life entity," together, according to the equation of regeneration of SHINSEI and the soul.

The sexual organs are the very important key and keyway for opening the door to the "Heaven." They are not only physically important, but also have spiritually special meaning. So, we must learn to use them in the right way. However, human beings do not understand the real meaning of them. We keep seeking sex, dominated by sexual desire, according to the "instinctive survival consciousnesses," but sexual organs are physically easy to be soiled and actually are soiled. Thus, the sexual organs are the symbol of undifferentiated sexual desire consciousness. But if we use them to express love, they will become most pure and noble.

The sexual organs of men exist along with the detoxification organs which excrete the toxins and wastes in the body, so men's

Chapter Three ☆ The Turning Point

sexual organs have both "impurity and purity," however, the sexual organs of women independently exist in the center of the detoxification organs and are separated from them. I think it means this. Women are the ones shouldering the role and the responsibility to accomplish the evolution of the spiritual consciousness entity and the evolution of the body, and men have stronger sexual desire consciousness, are more dominant than women, and try to expand the territory of the species by sexual relationship with women.

You can see the same behaviors in the animal kingdom. The male constantly conducts marking by pheromone contained in the urine, to display the territory of domination to other males.

The sexual organs of men are the termination of the excretion as a result of the dietary desire consciousness of water, which is the guard of the earth, and the starting point of the sexual desire consciousness. So, you could say that the desire exists in the most unclean point physiologically. The roots of all evil in history have derived from undifferentiated sexual desire consciousness of men. So, you could say that the sexual organs would become "the most impure things" if we do not know how to seek or how to use them. However, they will be "the most pure and noble things" in the spiritual world if we devote ourselves to learn how to treat them correctly based on love of SHINSEI unity, not with instinct of the earth star.

The two opposite things, which are love and desire, co-exist in the sexual organs, based on the "rule of entropy relativity," and those are the core of the life ethics. So we will be embarrassed in the "Heaven," the world for couples, if we treat them incorrectly. In reality, there are many married couples and love couples who have sorrow and ONSHU because they have mismatched key and keyway, however, if we try to keep going forward with spiritual evolution, step by step, we will surely meet the ideal partner, eventually, if we do not give up.

The spiritual world is not the one for Self-satisfaction or narcissism, and, of course, there is no mirror to reflect our own joy and pleasure. Since freedom and love penetrate the spiritual world of a higher spiritual dimension, the purpose and value to exist in that world is only for making others happy, so it will be very important how much you can accept love and how free your consciousness is to transform yourself, no matter what others wish. For example, if someone you love doesn't like your appearance, you can easily change your appearance to please them, without hesitation. It will be an important way of life to increase your own freedom by giving love to others more than to yourself. Therefore, it doesn't matter how good-looking or beautiful you are in this world, the material world, because appearances in this world have no meaning in the spiritual world, and in fact we will just be ashes when we die and are cremated. But if you are mentally a beauty of a higher spiritual dimension, the phenomena world in the spiritual world would be beautiful also.

The spiritual dimension will be determined by how you expand your capacity of love to accept and how much freedom you will gain. Since the spiritual consciousness entity is confined to the physical body, it is impossible to obtain the complete freedom of your spirit by your Self-effort. To exercise love, you need a partner as the object of love. After all, when you graduate from the earth star by the pair system between a woman and a man, you will be able to obtain true freedom. It means that you can be free only by giving love, so, the more you enlarge your capacity of love to accept, the more your freedom will increase. To love is to understand, to understand is to accept. This is the means to increase your capacity of love to accept. And when you can gain more love, then even though difficult things or hardships may happen to you in this world, you will feel that they have become smaller and are not a big deal anymore.

Since the person who is dominated by the values in this world, he/she would have an ugly and poor mind of lower spiritual dimension, as would a person who is narcissistic and caught up in the form and appearance by dominating in the category of appearance called the body. Then that person will become a poor and weak spiritual consciousness entity with degraded and inconvenient love, and will go to the unpleasant spiritual world.

In order to achieve Self-completion of true Self-Enlightenment, you should surpass the blind spot of the Mobius loop in the "vertical love" and the "horizontal love" by the way of life of PARAREVO, and achieve the Self-completion of integrated love personality formation of vertical and horizontal love. With this concept of Self-Enlightenment based on the theory of PARAREVO, it becomes possible to manifest the perfect collaboration world without dispute, struggle, domination, and exploitation.

3-56. Chakras are "spiritual organs" to integrate the soul and the body

The main cause of disease in mind and body is the integrity of the spiritual consciousness entity, chakras, and the body. This originated in the role and the mechanism of the chakras. Chakras are the "spiritual organs" which integrate the soul and the body. These are invisible and exist in everyone. However, if we do not use them, it is same as not existing. So, if we do not take care of our chakras, they will eventually become slow, unbalanced and blocked, and will become nonfunctional. While we are dominated by the desire consciousness of the body and continue to live as we are now, in the terrestrial life, there is no inconvenience or difficulty to live even though we ignore the presence of chakras. However, if we want to graduate from the earth star by releasing the physical domination and directing to the spiritual evolution, we have no choice but to activate and use our chakras.

The first life activity when we are born in this world is breathing, and our life starts when we give our first cry with exhalation, also our life ends when we breathe our last breath with inhalation. The chakras play a role the same as the respiratory organs, to breathe elementary primes for the spiritual consciousness entity to exist eternally. The mechanism of physical respiration is the system to take the oxygen from respiratory organs such as the nose, mouth, and skin, to the internal body, change the energy by the physiological mechanism, and release carbon dioxide from inside the body.

In order to sustain the soul, eternally, we should provide for the mechanism to derive the life force by the rule of the relative original power. The mechanism that makes it possible for the spiritual consciousness entity to exist eternally, directs us to complete our life as the relative subjectivity and our death as the relative objectivity, synchronically and simultaneously, based on the idea called the rule of "Sokushin Jourei." This means that it doesn't matter what

Chapter Three ☆ The Turning Point

you were or what you did in your life so far, but only this moment is memorized on your spiritual consciousness entity and determines which spiritual dimension your soul will go, and makes it possible to sustain the creation of the energy by the mechanism which is the same with respiration.

Chakra means the "rounded wheel" in Sanskrit, and it opens outwardly like a trumpet. Inside the wheel are several more wheels around the outer rings. Each chakra rotates with the breathing systems. They absorb energy by left rotation, and release it by right rotation. The common theory is that the spiritual consciousness entity breathes cosmic energy (free energy, prana, or chi) through the chakras. However, with the definition in the theory of PARAREVO, this energy wave is the dark energy which is created by the relative original power with SHINSEI, the "relative universal original power," and the whole creator world of the universe, and exists broadly in the universe according to each spiritual dimension. *The universe is the world of dark energy, which is the SHINSEI integration consciousness world and is integrated by the "relative universal original power." The spiritual consciousness entity breathes this dark energy depending on each spiritual dimension.*

Each chakra has its own role and energy wave to breathe, according to its location. They are located mainly in seven places, forming a line up the center of the body. Now, I will explain the role of those seven chakras based on the PARAREVO theory.

The first chakra, "Muladhara" is the primitive chakra and extremely vital energy wave, and breathes the material wave, the first "Ether entity" that is a lower spiritual dimension and red in color. This chakra connects the relative wave with the mineral world which is the first "Ether entity." The second "Suadhisthara" chakra connects the relative wave with the plant world which is the second "Ether entity," and the third "Manipura" chakra connects the relative wave with the animal world which is the third "Ether entity," and they integrate the energy wave of each body by directing it to the soul. The fourth chakra, "Anahata," exists in the space between the physical wave and the mental wave, and breathes the energy wave of the spiritual dimension of the "Astral entity." The fifth "Vishuddha" chakra connects the relative original power with the world of spirit which is mental entity, the sixth "Ajna" chakra connects the relative original power with the world of "Enlightened Spirit" which is the "Causal entity," and the seventh "Sahasrara" chakra connects the relative original power with SHINSEI and the spirit world which is the "Monad entity," and they integrate the energy wave of the soul directing to SHINSEI.

Like this, chakras have led the evolutionary process according to the "principle of dimensional integration," always directing the body and the mind to the higher direction by breathing the dark energy which is the spiritual energy created in the universe as elementary prime, by the "relative universal original power" based on free love. As the nutritional value of the body is different based on what you eat, the nutritional value of the soul would be different based on the spiritual dimension of the dark matter you breathe. Therefore, since chakras are released from the physical domination and activated by *the degree of acceptance of love and freedom,* activation and release of chakras have played the role as the guide in the evolutionary process.

The color and brightness of the aura is determined by the

Chapter Three ☆ The Turning Point

activated condition of each chakra, so a person whose "Muladhara" chakra and "Suadhisthara" chakra are dysfunctional, causing the integration of the mind and the body to become extremely imbalanced, is dominated by primitive material and sexual desire, and will have a dusky, muddy red aura.

Each person has a different way to see Chakras and auras. Since Chakras and auras are emphasized depending on the person's spiritual dimension, the spiritual dimension of the person who responds to Chakras is the most important, so a fixed idea is unnecessary because how the person see Chakras and auras changes, depending on the consciousness of the person, every moment.

A person, whose "Manipura" chakra, which is located in the solar plexus, is blocked, has a dirty yellow aura. The person whose "Sahasrara" chakra is dysfunctional resulting in schizophrenia and the energy is leaking from the burst part, has a dark blue-purple aura.

As you can see in the religious paintings and sculptures, there are golden shining halos surrounding the religious figures, so the relationship between chakras and aura is corresponding closely with the spiritual dimension. Activating the chakras makes it possible to manifest the individual art which makes the aura bright and shining and gives energy to the life, and manifests infinite individual art and revels in the spiritual life.

The spiritual consciousness entity, which is a higher dimension than materials, is originally free existence, so it has been the mystery of the mental world, including religions, why and by what mechanism the soul stays in the body, the material of lower dimension. The buttons of the soul, chakras, spread through the buttonhole of the body. So the condition the soul wears the prisoner uniform, called the body, which is our shape and appearance is forced to be inconvenient. The chakras go through the body, from back to front, like a button. When our body dies, the soul is released from the body in order, starting from the first chakra "Muladhara," by removing the buttons and taking off the clothes like butterfly flies from the chrysalis.

The degree of restriction of each chakra is different depending on the strength of the physical domination for the spiritual consciousness entity by desire and persistence of the body, then the spiritual life starts after the soul is released from the body.

The first chakra "Muladhara" is released from the physical domination of male prostate and female womb, however, if a person has strong material and sexual desire and persistent in money, or resentment of love, it will take a longer time to release that chakra.

The second chakra "Suadhisthara" is released from the physical domination of male gonads and female ovaries. However, if a person has strong sexual desire consciousnesses such as status and reputation desire, or has strong resentment and persistence toward sexual desire and lust by being dominated by undifferentiated sexual desire, it will also take a longer time to release.

The third chakra "Manipura" is released from the physical domination of a pancreatic islet "Langerhans," however, if a person has persistence and ONSHU in the material desire of strong dietary desire consciousness, it will be extremely difficult to release.

"Anahata" the fourth chakra is released from the physical domination of the thymus, however, if a person has experienced

Chapter Three ☆ The Turning Point

anxiety and fear, faced a strange or incurable disease such as an autoimmune disease, or has ONSHU toward illness and fear by shouldering traumas such as an insecure feeling toward illness and people or social phobia, it is tightly closed and difficult to release.

The fifth "Vishuddha" chakra is released from the physical domination of the thyroid, however, if a person has made mistakes in use of logos, emitting words of unpleasant emotions, created the Demon's world inside himself/herself with violence words, and committed Self-injury by Self-hatred and Self-denial, his/her chakra is closed and will be difficult to release.

"Ajna" the sixth chakra is released from the physical domination of the Pituitary Gland, however, a person who has ONSHU of resentment and bitterness toward the relationship with parents, siblings or marital relationship and other human relationship; it is closed and will not be released.

"Sahasrara" the seventh chakra is released last from the physical domination of the pineal gland. Since the pineal gland is the terminal organ in which physical world desires have been accumulated throughout the entire evolutional process, at the moment the soul is separated from the pineal gland, it will completely release from the body, and the soul will be born to the spiritual world.

3-57. Release of chakras and spiritual dimensions

A person, who has great persistence and a lingering attachment to the body and the physical world benefits, has very strongly bound chakras. If the chakras, as the button to connect the soul and the body are tightly closed, the chakras themselves will not function well and we will be physically dominated with unpleasant feelings, and the soul will be forced to an inconvenient condition. When we fall into that situation, because of unpleasant feelings, according to the physical domination by the "instinctive survival consciousnesses," it takes a long time for the soul to be released from the physical body, and it will lead to unfortunate results.

The ideal death is when the soul, the spiritual consciousness entity, senses the physical death instantaneously, and can release the physical domination immediately and leave the body. However, those whose chakras have been tightly closed by the physical domination and who lived their life being dominated by status, reputation, and materials, with the value of the physical world benefits, will find it spiritually difficult to deliver the soul to the spiritual world at the time of disembodiment, and it will be the hardest for the soul at the last moment of life.

The terrestrial life, the spiritual consciousness entity, has been tamed by the physical dominating structure, the "instinctive survival consciousnesses," by the genetic domination throughout history, and has been enslaved by being addicted to the desires and pleasures of the body. As a result of trying to gain the excessive physical world benefits and momentary values for others, to increase the things we will eventually lose, we invite the sad result that the soul still remains on the material world despite of the death of the physical body.

The relationship between chakras and the body for those who have regret, obsession, and ONSHU in this world, is like the relationship between firmly rusted bolts and nuts, which were rusted because of desires and ONSHU. In such a situation, even though the soul wishes to be released from the body and become free as soon as possible, the disembodiment will be impossible because of the strong physical domination.

Chakras integrate the soul and the body, and form harmony and order of physiological functions for the mind and the body. The moment the soul dwelled in bacteria, the primitive life entity, chakras started to function and it began life as a primitive organism of the combination of the spirit and the body, although, it only had a mouth to ingest food, the intestines to create energies by digesting and absorbing food, and the anus for excretion. The chakra of the primitive life entity was only a model for the "Muladhara," which was the first and base chakra.

Following the vector of the universe, the spiritual consciousness entity has directed to the spiritual evolution, and the intention, which was the mental energy, to the genes through the chakras, has come together in the evolutional process of the soul and the body. The feelings and sensitivity which is beyond the physical senses, becomes the mental energy, so human beings evoke the genetic consciousness of the brain through chakras and the axis line. Then we spread the intracerebral hormone substance to the central nerves as neurotransmitters, and transmit to the genes after passing the ion channels for each cell. For example, when the mind becomes excited with uplifted feelings and sensitivity, the intracerebral hormone substances, such as dopamine and adrenaline, flow from the brain to the central nerves as faint electric current, working on DNA code, and becoming a catalyst for cells.

Chakras directly connect to hormones, transcend the brain domination, and provide the energy and information according to each role and responsibility, independently, separated from the brain. Physical evolution will be possible by the mutual effect integrated to the Trinity of chakras, nervous system, and endocrine system, and DNA has been programming the result of the evolution into the chromosome in the cell nucleus as a blueprint of the genetic code.

By the integrated work of the relative original power of the consciousness, chakras, and hormone system, it is determined whether the environmental adaptation could be done or not. If there is no environmental adaptation ability, we will become sick and our lives will be ruined, or if there is environmental adaptation ability, we will overcome sickness and accomplish evolution.

Thus, *the onset of a disease and treatment are led to the integrity of the consciousness, chakras, and the hormonal system. The environmental adaptation ability for the new evolution will be determined whether it directs to the soul according to the "principle of dimensional integration" based on the rule of "spirit is subjective and body is objective," or it directs to the body according to the "principle of dimensional domination" based on the rule of "body is subjective and spirit is objective."*

3-58. Dysfunction of chakras occurs by unpleasant feelings

Certain conditions in the chakra, such as the dysfunction of the "Anahata" chakra, are often found in people who suffer from immune deficiency disease. This might have happened when the person was still a fetus in the mother's womb and the mother had

Chapter Three ☆ The Turning Point

unpleasant feelings such as anxiety and fear during her pregnancy. A condition such as this would affect the chakra located in the underdeveloped chest of the fetus. This would also happen to a person who had experienced extreme anxiety and fear during his/her personality formation history in this world.

When we encounter a situation of insecurity and fear, we react, unconsciously and instantly, putting our hand on our chest, so it shows that the fourth chakra is deeply affected by the feelings of anxiety and fear, and we unconsciously try to protect our "Anahata" chakra from significant obstacles, which might harm it. And when we feel greatly relieved, it is said in Japanese that we stroke down the chest. It also, physically, has an important influence on the hormonal system called the thymus, which manages our immune system.

Feelings of anger are related to the second chakra, and it has significant influence on the hormone systems such as the prostate and gonads for men, and ovaries and uterus for women. We often use expressions such as "gut-wrenching feeling" and "boiling with anger" to connect the position of chakras. The emotional energies of anger and vigor are accumulated in the second chakra of the lower abdomen. The sexual hormone has the most significant connection with the sexual desire, and it converts the dominating desire into battle energy, so that even though gentle male herbivorous animals, during the mating season, develop intense confrontations with each other in order to acquire females.

The feeling of sadness is related to the third chakra, and has a significant influence on the pancreas and adrenal glands. There is a close relationship among feelings, chakras, and the hormonal systems, and they constantly work to try to protect our lives. Women's menstruation, menopausal disorder, menopausal depression, and breast and uterine cancers are caused by the hormonal mutual interaction between the second chakra and the estrogen.

All changes which have occurred in our body have corresponded to evolution by environmental adaptation, according to the "principle of dimensional integration" by the Trinity of the consciousness, chakra, and the hormonal system. At the same time, chakras have evolved with the evolution of the body.

In the beginning, the first chakra "Muladhara," which had controlled the primitive dietary desire and the sexual desire, had been used for both functions. According to evolution by the sexual differentiation, the second chakra "Suadhisthara" came into control of the sexual hormones. The third chakra "Manipura" controls the insulin of beta cells in the islets of Langerhans in the pancreas, and by integrating the digestive system. The fourth, "Anahata" chakra has integrated the immune system by connecting the thymus, and achieved environmental adaptation from Homo habilis to Homo sapiens, and the evolution to intellectual life entity. The fifth chakra "Vishuddha" formed the thyroid gland and the vocal cords and achieved evolution rapidly by starting to use languages as a communication tool, and the sixth chakra "Ajna" formed the brain hypothesis and evolved to advanced thoughtful life entity. The seventh chakra "Sahasrara" formed the pineal gland, and achieved evolution to the intellectual life entity which integrated the entire body together with the spiritual evolution, so that they prove that the chakras and the hormonal systems evolved together.

3-59. The time required for disembodiment and spiritual dimensions

The time required for chakras to be released from the body, and the soul completely freed, is important because it will tell how we have organized our personality formation history in this life. The amount of time it takes for chakras to be released from the body will determine the level of spiritual dimension that the soul will go. The faster they are released, the higher the dimension they will attain.

This separation time is not related to how you die. Whether you die by accident, by disease, by natural disaster, or by aging, will not have any influence on the time required. The required time for the disembodiment and the level of spiritual dimension will be determined by the releasing degree of chakras from the desire and ONSHU of the physical domination. The chakras of a child who died young are immature and innocent, and do not have strong influence by physical domination, so their soul immediately leaves the body and returns to the spiritual world.

It is hard to say that living long in this world is a good life. I think it is more important to stay free from the physical domination, so we should keep the button holes of the body, the prisoner uniform, loosened for the soul. Even if we encounter sudden death, if we are always prepared to loosen the buttons and the button holes and be ready to take off our cloth, immediately without any lingering or persisting attachment to the uniform, then the spiritual dimension to which our souls go is higher than the person who does not prepare anything and their buttons and button holes are tightly fixed like rusty bolts and nuts, deeply attached with the physical world and ONSHU, their souls will not be able to achieve the disembodiment for a long time.

The higher spiritual dimension we will be able to go to when our chakras are freed from the physical domination without any lingering or persisting attachment or ONSHU at the time of death, and the place our souls will go is the place where the path of emotions is opened to love and joy, and will be able to enjoy the individual art. Thus, the condition of released chakras based on the *acceptance degree of love and freedom* determines the required time for the disembodiment, however, which spiritual dimension we go to should be Self-determined.

The time limit for the soul to go to the spiritual world is approximately within eight hours in this world time after physical death. The "required time" I mention here is a statistical supposition from my experiences with my clients in my clinic. If it takes more than eight hours, the soul will be tied to this world and become lingering and haunting, and the evil spirits will come and hold your soul requiring it to remain in this world as it is. When it is released from the physical domination within eight hours and completes the disembodiment, other spirits, such as those of ancestors, will come and together go to the spiritual world of the earth star, which is the intangible substantial world.

When the soul is released from the physical domination within 21 seconds in this world time, spirituality being in the "Causal entity dimension" will welcome the soul, and according to the equation of regeneration of SHINSEI and the soul, based on the "rule of change by birth and re-birth," will proceed by the love pair system of SHINSEI unity of good-natured men and good-natured women. This can release the "rule of reincarnation" based on the "rule of spiritual causality," and leave from the earth star, the prison planet, permanently, achieves the spiritual evolution to the SHINSEI integrated life entity of a newer universal dimension, and will sublimates to the higher spiritual dimension together with pure white light.

The one and only purpose of life in this world is *the preparation period for graduating from the earth star, the prison planet, and to live the spiritual life forever. It is not for remaining on the earth star according to the "rule of reincarnation."*

The level in the spiritual world is led to the Self-management with Self-determination and Self-completion by Self-responsibility, based on the "rule of freedom." The universe strictly secures *the principle of Self-responsibility based on the "principle of nonaggression and nonintervention"* in order to guarantee the "rule of freedom." There is no salvation by others in the "rule of the universe." So, as I have mentioned many times before, there is no meaning to ceremony or prayers to God.

3-60. Chakra adjustment methods of resuscitation by Self-reliance and reliance upon others

For a method to release and activate the chakras on your own, there is a breathing method called Anapanasati (mindfulness of breathing) of Buddha since ancient times. However, the method based on the PARAREVO theory is *a powerful and strong SHINSEI breathing method to connect universe, human, and earth perpendicularly, and pass through the axis line of chi from "Sahasrara" chakra and link to SHINSEI, vertically.*

Logos of the "universal phoneme" is the one to be integrated according to the "rule of the universe." This "universal phoneme" of logos has never existed in the past, even in the Tibetan Buddhism and yoga. Since it winds the IRE energy (integrated relative energy), in which the three elements are united, around the joints between chakras and the body by the power of SHINSEI integration consciousness, it would never make negative-type mental disorder with Kundalini syndrome, such as schizophrenia appear and cause personality destruction by destroying the "Sahasrara" chakra and "Ajna" chakra, which often happens by primitive methods like Kundalini yoga.

These releasing methods of chakras, the adjustment method of resuscitation, it poured lubricating oil amrita, on rusty bolts and nuts, loosened chakras which were tightly closed by physical domination, and let it start to exercise, and gradually activate the rotary motion and adjust consciousness, respiration, and rhythm. And each chakra has its own effective logos to work well.

Logos means reason and rational, so the reason I call it logos is that it is the tool (instrument), and it can become a dangerous weapon if used incorrectly. If we just concentrate on techniques such as meditation and breathing, like some mysticism or theosophy, we may fall into Self-satisfaction or a fantasy game of Self-intoxication. So, we should follow an undeniable existentialism based on the way of life of PARAREVO, achieve Self-Enlightenment and spiritual evolution by ourselves based on the equation of spiritual evolution, which is to release our own ONSHU by loving the existing ONSHU,

Chapter Three ☆ The Turning Point

raise *the degree of acceptance of love and freedom of consciousness,* and ascend the steps of the spiritual dimension one by one. It will certainly release chakras.

If you wish to rely upon others, there is a method to release chakras by the person of SHINSEI integration consciousness who is skilled and experienced IRE adjustment technique of chakras resuscitation, with inducement and semi-force. In any case, we should master the method to release chakras and attain proficiency by spending time and achieving Self-Enlightenment and spiritual evolution under firm guidance.

3-61. The level of releasing chakras determines the direction of spiritual dimensions

The rhythm adjustment of chakras coordinates and repairs the spin period and the rotation direction of dysfunctional chakras, and this is the method to recover the periodic balance of the rotation by Self-reliance and reliance on others. With the rhythm adjustment, it aims to accomplish the original role and responsibility for chakras.

In the spiritual world, there are many spiritual dimensions from the lower dimension of evil spirit, such as one which committed murder, or entrapped spirit of a suicide, to a spiritually awakened person in the higher spiritual dimension. Various spiritual waves from the spiritual world traveled freely on the earth as electric waves on the ground, so since chakras are the spiritual antenna, we are always influenced by some kind of spiritual waves regardless of good or bad. This spiritual wave derives the external relative original power based on the spirit and mind.

Chakras play the role of antenna, to catch the spiritual waves, and those spiritual waves would have a great influence mentally on the spiritual consciousness entity through chakras. For example, if people's chakras which are deeply connected with sexuality are dysfunctional, it causes serious mental disorders such as schizophrenia, and those people often hold some problems in their family relationship such as between the parent-child and the siblings, and easily fall into unnatural sexual relationships and sexual assault, like incest. They imposed a strong shock on "Muladhara" chakra and "Suadhisthara" chakra which connected with the genitals during their developing period, so that the sexual energy blew up toward "Sahasrara" chakra, located on the top of the head, through the axis line of chi, like a volcano erupting, resulting in the dysfunction of the "Sahasrara" chakra, which was the center of the spiritual antenna, and also destroying the integrity of the mind and the body. As a result, the spiritual waves of the lower dimension jump in without permission, through broken chakras, and many of them reflected to the brain, causing confusion inside the brain, which will bring on delusion and illusion. Those conditions are not related to his/her personality or spirituality.

As you can see by this example, when chakras become dysfunctional for any reason, the result is often sexual deviation disorder, a condition similar to schizophrenia, and easily has unnatural sexual behavior such as homosexuals, and tends to have spiritual paranoia. Patients with schizophrenia and other mental disorders have significant problems in the subconscious mind based on the spirituality formation history, and their chakras are in an unbalanced or disorderly condition.

Chapter Three ☆ The Turning Point

We have experienced strong unpleasant feelings by the "rule of the relative original power" based on the spirit and mind and the spiritual waves in the lower dimension. At that time, the chakras are affected adversely, and become dysfunctional, spinning reversely, and we fall into mental disorder. Abnormal condition of chakras give negative impact on the spirituality (the soul) and the personality (the mind), and induce spiritual disorders, with evil spirits, by the relative original power. As a result, the person suffers from incurable and rare diseases of unknown cause, and it would be impossible to treat with modern medicine, such as malignant tumors and internal illnesses like autoimmune diseases.

The condition of the chakras has a great impact on us mentally and physically. For example, the consciousnesses of a person whose chakras are spinning reversely, is inclined to go to time-slipping into the past, always dominated in the past, and is in a mental condition which tends to have victim delusions and illusions like dementia or schizophrenia. On the other hand, if the spin speed of chakras is fast, the consciousness of a person tends to go to time-slipping into the future, easily evoking anxiety or fear of the future, find it hard to sleep because of restlessness and stimulation of the EEG, and often show mental disorders such as depression. When our consciousness shifts to the past or the future, it awakens not the memories of the brain but the memories of the soul depending on the direction and the speed of the spin of the chakras. So we are able to live in the present existentially and comfortably when our body is well balanced and integrated to the spiritual consciousness entity.

Also, according to the releasing degree and ability of the

chakras, the spiritual dimension in the consciousness level will be significantly different. Let me explain this using the example of radio or TV antennas. The person whose chakras are like a transistor radio antenna in the local broadcast area, might spend his/her lifetime in their place of birth without raising any sensitivity or feelings, not having any interest in anything, living from hand to mouth, and leave this world like a fossil of history. A person whose chakras are like local TV antenna live a life with an interest in the cities and the provinces, and a person whose chakras are like the national broadcasting station antenna live a life with an interest in the nations, a person whose chakras are like the BS or satellite antenna live a life with an interest in the world, and a person who has chakras like the universal antenna lives a life with an interest in the intangible substantial world and the universe beyond the earth star.

Thus, the releasing degree in the functional capabilities of the chakras determines the height and the size of the interests in the existing purpose for life and the values in the individual purpose, from the individual dimension to the family, the ethnic group, the national, and the world dimension.

3-62. Verification of sexual integration and sexual anomaly

The personality and the nature of human beings are determined by *the sexual integration and sexual anomaly,* and there are basically four different types of sexual integration and deviation of the spiritual consciousness entity.

Chapter Three ☆ The Turning Point

When the physical body is a male the nature is classified into "masculine positive nature" and "masculine negative nature." And when the physical body is a female, it is classified into "feminine positive nature" and "feminine negative nature." So combined, there are four major patterns between man and woman.

A man of the "masculine positive nature" is the one whose integrated life entity is well-matched as a man for his body and soul. A man of the "masculine negative nature" is the one whose body is a male but the soul inside is a female or very close to a female. In this case, you could say that he has mismatching integration deviation life entity. A woman of the "feminine negative nature" is the one whose integrated life entity is well-matched as a woman for her body and the soul, and a woman of the "female positive nature" is the one whose body is a female but the soul inside is a male or very close to a male. In this case, you also could say that she has mismatching integration deviation life entity.

It is no exaggeration to say that this integrity and the deviation determine the nature and the personality, and also determine the consciousness, motivation, behavior, fundamental intention, and orientation in life. So, those who have a remarkably unbalanced nature the sexual integrity and relativity are called transgender or sexual integration disorder. Especially, the person whose spiritual consciousness entity is transgender has a totally mismatched soul and body. Homosexual women and men are the ones whose sexual integration is not in order. I think it would be caused by genetic disorder, such as the physical memories of incest and sexual assault inside their genes.

Homosexuals, as the nature of sexual integration disorder, are manifestations of sexual anomalies, according to the "rule of the genetic chain" based on the physical causality, and the transgender persons are also manifestations of sexual deviation disorders, according to the "rule of reincarnation" based on the spiritual causality. Those who have sexual integration disorders are the ones who have some sexual problems and difficulties in their personality formation history and genetic chain. And they often have the personality problems accompanied with the dysfunction of chakras, and connote sexual disorders by sexual disgrace of lineage as wounds of genes. The major causes of sexual integration disorders connote undifferentiated sexual impulse, such as chimpanzee bonobos, which conduct sexual relationship actively, even among the same sex. So their sexual differentiation is underdeveloped, and their spiritual evolution is not advanced yet.

Transgender people are the innate sexual deviation disorders, which the spiritual consciousness entity, the soul, complies with the cause, problem and task based on the Self-determination, according to the "rule of reincarnation" based on the rule of "spirit is subjective and body is objective." And the sexual integration disorders are the acquired sexual deviation disorders, caused by genetic domination, based on the rule of "body is subjective and soul is objective."

Since both of them unbalance the integrity of the mind and the body, we could say that basically they are due to the functional disorder of chakras.

3-63. The methods to surpass and transcend sexual anomalies

One of the basic ideas of the depth psychology is this: Throughout the evolutionary history, the sexual deviation structure has differentiated into the male nature and the female nature. This structure exists in everybody as a fatal nature of the sexual separation life entity. This mechanism becomes a major factor to prevent the evolution of sexual differentiation to a higher dimension.

The orientation and value of the consciousness, which determines the individual mental entity, is fixed based on the sexual integrity and deviation. Also, there exist many details and wide-ranging integrity and deviation patterns in the four major divided patterns, by the "rule of balance." So, it will be the important concept of life to make Self-effort to direct the sexual separation life entity, well-balanced, moderate, and neutral, and bring it close to your own sexual integrated life entity.

In order to do so, it will be important to manifest the ideal pair system of love as the individual art of the individual mind entity, and have the common existing purpose of life for graduating from the earth star with SHINSEI as the common denominator, and with individuality as the molecule, based on the life of PARAREVO.

Those who have sexual deviation disorders should make Self-effort to direct to the integration of the mind and the body based on the rule of "spirit is subjective and body is objective," without criticism or evaluation of others, and to choose the way of life as the individual entity. Even though you are homosexual or transgender, you should realize that you are the one who made the choice of your sex by yourself, so you must accept yourself unconditionally based on the theory of PARAREVO, and achieve Self-completion of life as the individual art.

3-64. Chakras will disappear in the "intangible world"

There is an existing purpose for chakras of the spiritual consciousness entity, the soul. It is working as the respiratory organ to breathe the cosmic energy, as the integration organ to connect the soul and the body relatively, and as the receiving organ to catch various waves in the space from the material wave to the spiritual wave. Chakras are essential for the life entity as long as we live in this world, but they have no purpose after disembodiment and the soul leaves for the spiritual world. At that time they are assimilated to the spiritual consciousness entity and disappear naturally.

This is the same as the prenatal life in which the fetus needs the placenta and umbilical code in the mother's womb, but in the ground life after birth they are of no use and will disappear naturally. Since chakras are the spiritual organ attached to the soul, they are necessary during the physical domination period on the earth star. However, they lose the role and the responsibility in the spiritual world and disappear.

Since chakras are the spiritual organ existing in the soul, they are not seen or understood in the material civilization, so it is difficult for many people to accept their existence. As long as we just survive physically in this world, we do not feel any inconvenience or difficulty without chakras, or the necessity and importance of them. However, recently, increasing numbers of people are seeking

Chapter Three ☆ The Turning Point

spiritual evolution and looking chakras over again seriously. In particular, more people feel that their body's existence is inconvenient after their spiritual evolution, to a certain extent, and are feeling somewhat out of place with their body.

Since we are preparing to go to the spiritual world, we must experience the integrated consciousness world of the universe beyond the body, and create the spiritual individual art while staying in this world. Otherwise, we are not able to do anything even if we go to the spiritual world, which is the world of SHINSEI integration consciousness. If we do not have the experience in this world, we are not able to understand. If we do not understand, we are not able to reach the confidence of the soul. If the soul is not certain, it does not reach to belief. Without belief, there is no courage. Without courage, there is no creation. If the experience and creation in this world is not necessary in the spiritual world, this world would lose the existing purpose and existing value, and if there is no purpose and value to exist, this world would be entirely meaningless and not necessary.

Even though we are integrated in free love after disembodiment, and sublimated to the spiritual world, if the soul is still at the extension line of habit of the physical domination experienced in this world, and selects the lower spiritual dimension in the astral zone, by itself, then it might exist in the inconvenient spiritual world. So, in order to make the most of chakras in this world and achieve spiritual evolution, we must experience and master the world of "SHINSEI integration consciousness." Nothing more exists than your spiritual consciousness entity has already experienced, also there is no existence or manifestation of anything more than that in the spiritual world.

In order to go to the "intangible substantial world," the "SHINSEI integration world," and revel in the individual art of joy by the relative original power based on free love, it is essential to activate and release chakras in this world, train IRE which is the world of SHINSEI integration consciousness beyond the body, and acquire transcendental ability beyond the body.

People who live a life of PARAREVO can create the integrated relative energy, IRE, handling a human's body freely from a distant place through chakras, and are able to perform a rhythmical adjustment of the mind and the body, and cure various illnesses. As a result, they are enjoying the creative individual art of gratitude and happiness, by awakening their own consciousness.

3- 65. The relative wave based on the spiritual dimension and the "principle of the relative original power"

By the power of SHINSEI integration consciousness, it will be possible to make the human body push, knock down, pull toward or pull up freely. But how can we do such things?

In the universe, all things are forced to exist by the "relative universal original power," and everything exists based on the spiritual dimension. In order to make all this possible, there must be a mechanism to create some kind of power and energy in each spiritual dimension. All power and the source of energy are created or derived by the "rule of the relative original power" by the relative wave based on each spiritual dimension. By the "rule of the relative

Chapter Three ☆ The Turning Point

place in proportion," to each dimension, such as three dimensions, five dimensions, or seven dimensions, their power and energy are created or derived and function based on each spiritual dimension, according to the "rule of the relative original power."

The size and strength of the generating or deriving creation original power and the dimension of the energy wave would be different based on the relativity of things. For instance, the size and strength of the power and energy wave of plants is larger than minerals, animals are larger than plants, and human beings are larger than animals.

The existing consciousness based on each spiritual dimension would be different in the different qualitative energy, which is created or derived by the relative original power, such as speed and strength of fluid energy and fluid wave. If the qualitative energy of the inherent wave in relative things is different, it is difficult to create or derive the relative original power. It is also difficult to create fluid energy and fluid wave. So, it is easier to derive or create the strong relative original power when relative things are the same levels and dimensions.

For human beings, it will be easy to derive synergistic resonance phenomenon with other humans rather than with minerals, plants or animals. And it is possible to create or derive large fluid energy and fluid wave, so that the speed of the fluid transformation will be faster. Materials can move themselves eventually, however, since the qualitative energy in the spiritual dimension of the material itself is potentially lower, it takes a long time to connect to the relative wave and be resonant.

The same thing will happen to human beings. If the person's

qualitative energy is different, it will take a bit of time to resonate the energy with others, and in very few cases, like one out of thousands, there is a person who cannot feel any energy from others at all. It can be proven that such a person has strong sorrow and ONSHU in his/her personality formation history, and is extremely strong in fear and suspicion, suffering from mistrust. It could be said that those persons have the material level of the personality and stay in the lower spiritual dimension.

The spiritual dimension is composed of 7 major layers from the first "Ether entity" to the "Monad entity," and when the spirit goes to the higher spiritual dimension, there is less physical domination, so it is easier to connect the resonant wave to SHINSEI integration consciousness and will be converted faster to dynamic energy. By the "rule of the relative original power" based on the spirit and mind, a person who has higher personality of love and deep consciousness of sentiment can create the qualitative energy of the higher spiritual dimension than a person who has strong consciousness of the physical desire.

It will be possible to diagnose and verify easily the spirituality of the spiritual dimension connecting with the relative wave to the sentimental world and the personality dimension of that person, by the strength of the relative original power based on the spirit. By this rule, the criterion of the soul, which is hidden by the body, and the criterion of the personality, is clarified and it is possible to survey the spiritual dimension, no matter how you deceive or pretend, your spiritual consciousness entity hidden in the body will be revealed.

The releasing degree and activating degree of chakras are what control the receiving and the sending of the relative waves in the spiritual dimension, which were formed by the degree of acceptance of love and freedom of the consciousness, based on the spirituality formation history and the personality formation history.

3-66. Power of the collective consciousness by the relative original power

All things are forced to exist according to the relative wave, based on the spiritual dimension and the "rule of the relative original power," and people who are spiritually relative exchange the relative wave unconsciously through chakras, and exist with mutual interference by pulling each other. This phenomenon is called *the "rule of grouping."*

In the natural world, from the mineral world to bacteria, plants, insects and animals, all things are necessary to make groups with the same races even though nobody made such a rule. This is called *the power of collective consciousness by the relative original power.* We are directed to exchange the relative wave through chakras, unconsciously, and create various relations, organizations, and groups. When we go to the spiritual world after taking our clothes, the body, off, there is nothing to cover the soul. So, we form the same groups according to the spiritual dimension, and exist by being classified clearly from the "Astral plane" to the "Causal plane." In this world, since chakras of human beings are the easiest to be relative with the wave and create the relative original power with human beings, we make groups with other human beings and form the community.

The chakras of poorly natured people become relative with the wave of other poorly natured people, and those who are similar in temperament make organizations and groups with each other. Persons of admirable character exchange the relative wave by chakras with persons of similar admirable character, and will create their relationship. Religious organizations exchange the relative wave with chakras of the same "Astral middle level dimension" in their personality level, and create their organizations and groups. And also those with sexual integration disorders, such as homosexuals, exchange the relative wave by chakras and exist with similar groups. In the entertainment districts, the community is created by the people who have lonely spiritual dimension in their mind and their relative wave with chakras. Also residential areas would be different depending on each relative wave. They form in the natural flow, from uptown neighborhood of wealthy people to backstreet areas of poor people.

On the extension line of their spiritual dimension, the "intangible substantial world" exists. So even if they live in the gorgeous high society life, if they are greedy and poorly natured, they will go to the spiritual world of the collective consciousness group in the lower spiritual dimension such as where hungry ghosts live, and even though they live a poor life, if they are rich in mind, they will go to the world of the collective consciousness groups of suitable higher spiritual dimension. The spiritual world is the world without the body, and we are not able to cover and hide the mind and the soul, so that all things are manifested faithfully and it is the actual world without deception.

3-67. The relative original power and "Surprising phenomena"

Since the universe always directs to the higher spiritual dimension, if we would like to achieve spiritual evolution we should avoid the connection with ones in the lower dimension and not create the relative original power with them. For example, many religious groups and spiritual groups sell their goods of seal, altar, mantra, crystals and special stones such as tourmaline, titanium, or water, at very high prices with the explanation of unnatural theories as if they have divine help or special power.

In the relative original power between the materials, bodies, I admit to the existence of some kind of energy in the materials. It releases the oxygen dominating structure of atoms and molecules, and raises the power temporarily. I call this the "Surprising phenomena." However, they will lose the effectiveness, someday, by the "rule of balance" and the principle of environmental adaptation, because it is relatively impossible to create the energy constantly and permanently for merely the material dimension with the life dimension called cell. Also, goods raise the power in a moment, by the "Surprising phenomena" with the materials wave when we wear them, however, since those goods direct to form the harmony and the order based on the "rule of balance," they eventually lose the effectiveness and the efficacy by the environmental adjustment of the body. This is the fate of materials in the lower dimension, which is the same with health foods, health goods, and some kinds of medicines which appear like a comet but always disappear even though they temporarily become a boom.

Since the material waves in the lower dimension are not able to connect relatively with the spiritual waves in the higher dimension permanently, it is impossible to derive the relative original power on a permanent basis. Like the relationship between risk and drugs, when we always use drugs there are some risks, so when we continue to wear the goods, the material waves of lower dimension overstep the borderline of the risk and dominate the life entity of higher dimension, according to the "principle of dimensional domination," such as tourmalines and other crystals, are becoming harmful.

It would never really heal the soul of a higher dimension by using the five physical senses of the material dimension such as healing music, aromatherapy, color therapy, and massages. For instance, the range of our hearing sense in the body is limited to the range of 20Hz to 20kHz, however, the range of the soul exists in much higher wavelengths, so it is the same thing that the radio or the television is nothing but noise if the frequency does not match.

Since in the spiritual world, the spirits are exchanging their thoughts by the spiritual element as their medium, and the intention is immediately transmitted without words. People who live the way of PARAREVO always seek the healing world of the soul beyond the materials, and make Self-effort to manifest the existential human healing, which they exchange by the spirit wave of the higher spiritual dimension without any words, sounds, colors, and scents, and heal each other by just being there and transcending the material wave.

Chapter Three ☆ The Turning Point

3-68. The purpose of the true spirituality formation by Self-completion

To achieve Self-completion of the true personality formation means to achieve Self-completion of the ideal personality formation of love. In doing so, we should integrate the "vertical love" of the blind spot of the Mobius loop in the parent-child relationship, and the "horizontal love" of the blind spot of the Mobius loop in the sibling relationship and marital relationship in this world, by releasing and surpassing the sorrow and ONSHU vertically and horizontally by the way of life of PARAREVO. We should accomplish the role and responsibility of the individual purpose to graduate from the earth star, and manifest our precious valuable life as the individual art, and make Self-effort toward the realization of the entire purpose of the collaboration world.

The purpose for Self-completion of the true spirituality formation is to release the physical domination and build the foundation for the creation and manifestation of the individual art of eternal sustainable joy in the spiritual world, based on free love. The equation for Self-completion of the true spirituality formation is explained like this. If you would like to become a person with an admirable character, you should actively involve yourself with people in a higher personality dimension, and then you will inevitably become a person of character in the higher spiritual dimension. If you want to be a human in the poor and lower dimension, you can be one by being involved with those who are in the poor and lower dimension.

Our personality will be formed by the spiritual dimension of those we are involved with, such as our parents, siblings, and friends. Our spirituality will be formed, relatively, by the spiritual dimension of the "spirituality entity" with whom we are involved. The "spirituality entity" means the existence of a spiritual being in the spiritual world after separating from the body. Those spiritual beings exist in many layers of the spiritual dimension, from ghost spirit of the "Astral entity" in the lower dimension to Enlightened Spirit of the "Causal entity" in the higher dimension. In order to complete the spirituality formation for directing to the higher spiritual dimension in this world, *we should release our own ONSHU by loving the ONSHU according to the "principle of dimensional integration" by internal separation, based on the PARAREVO theory.*

We must create the relative original power, actively, with the spiritual beings of the higher spiritual dimension, and direct to the way of life of PARAREVO, which exercises the consciousness of love, and conduct our behaviors with the motivation of goodness. The most important thing to do this is to release your own ONSHU, individually. Since the three layer structure of the triangle system of SHINSEI, the soul, and the body, is the core of ONSHU of the individual life entity, it is necessary to release the "instinctive remaining consciousnesses," such as material desire, status desire, and reputation desire, and then try to relate with the higher spiritual dimension.

The spirituality entity of the higher spiritual dimension will relate with unselfish and Self-sacrificing people of the same level, however, the spirituality entity of the lower spiritual dimension relates, relatively, to selfish people with the hypocrisy of Self-satisfaction who have strong physical world benefits.

Chapter Three ☆ The Turning Point

There are various spiritual waves coming and going freely as electric waves, from the spiritual world which is the "intangible substantial world," and, especially the spiritual waves in the lower dimension will come and go in the lowland area, overwhelmingly, according to the gravity domination.

The iron bar of the prison star, the earth star, is the gravity density of air, and this gravity is in inverse proportion to the level of the spiritual dimension. Because the gravity of air in the mountains is thinner than at ground level, there would be a higher spiritual wave than on flat ground. So, this explains why, since ancient times, people have worshiped in the high mountains. We cannot say whether it is good or bad, but, it is true that we live in this world under the influence of some kind of spiritual waves, unconditionally and unprotected.

3-69. The "principle of the relative original power" based on spirit and mind in the higher dimension

As we can see by the many symbolized places such as famous spots for suicide or accident, energy spots, and sacred places, even entertainment districts, it is the influence of the spiritual wave which exists at the same level spiritually and substantially, by connecting the relative wave in the same level of the spiritual dimension based on the "rule of grouping" and the "rule of the relative ground." The spot where accidents often happen is the place where the spiritual waves of those who died by accident are easy to be relative, and the spot where many people committed suicide is the place where the spiritual waves those who committed suicide are easy to be relative.

Usually, the things that happen in this world are directed by the cause, problem, and assignment which you had determined in the spiritual world, which is the phenomenon world of incarnation, so the personality is manifested as the relative phenomenon of the spirituality. The spirituality of a criminal exists behind the criminal, and the spirituality of a person murdered exists behind the murderer, since those are connecting the relative wave in the relation with a past life.

The spirituality of a good person exists behind the good person, and the spirituality of a bad person exists behind the bad person. This phenomenon is called *the "rule of the relative original power" based on spirit and mind.* In the spirit and mind, the mind represents the personality, and the spirit represents the spirituality being related to the personality, so that by the relative original power between the personality and the spirituality, the relative original power derives and the consciousness is exercised and directed to your behaviors based on the motivation.

The personality connotes in the emerging consciousness based on the personality formation history and exists as a habit of mind, and the spirituality connotes in the subconscious based on the spirituality formation history and exists as a habit of soul. Comparing this rule to a radio wave emitted from a broadcasting station, a channel, and an antenna, the waves emitted from each station corresponds to the spiritual wave emitted from the spiritual world of each spiritual dimension, chakras play the role of antenna which catch the spiritual waves like a regular antenna catches the broadcasting wave, and a channel corresponds to the spiritual dimension of each personality.

Chapter Three ☆ The Turning Point

Since personality and spirituality connect through chakras according to the spiritual dimension of the relative wave by the "rule of the relative original power" based on spirit and mind, it will be an important concept to raise the degree of acceptance of love and the freedom degree of the consciousness of the personality channel, raise the precision of chakras and the degree of releasing, and improve the spiritual dimension of the relative spirituality.

Since we all connote the "soul mind" and the "body mind" inside ourselves, it will be a significantly different life for us whether we relate with a person with whom we can invoke the "soul mind," or whether we relate with a person with whom we invoke the "body mind." Of course, it will have a greater impact on our life whether we relate with good spirit, or with evil spirit. For example, the personality formation history of a person who is easily caught up in occult shows and/or horror programs on TV is lacking in motherly love and causing personality destruction, or has possibly been spoiled by grand-parents because of discord between wife and mother-in-law.

The relative wave of the personality destruction entering the chakras connotes undifferentiated sexual desire consciousness of the poor spiritual dimension, has the tendency to be relative with ugly and nasty waves, and cause violent crimes by undifferentiated sexual impulse. Because of the lack of Self-integration, those people are not able to draw a line between false image in the virtual world and real image in the reality world. Consequently, they will connect with the relative wave in the poor personality and the poor spiritual dimension, and be directed to sexual disgrace, invoke the poor consciousness, and to be guided to violent crimes, spiritually, with ugly motivation. As a result, they are losing the nature of themselves and being induced to psychotic criminal behavior, and after committing a crime they come to their senses, fall into fear because of the seriousness of what they have done, and run away, because the spirituality which achieved the criminal purpose left from the person's mind.

The personality formation history of a person who has a strong sexual desire and indulges in masturbation by invoking the consciousness in sexual fantasy, and who also has a strong physical world desire and undifferentiated sexual desire consciousness, which are inserted as a wound of genes. Those persons are easy to invoke the undifferentiated sexual habit and sexual impulse because of their sexual desires which are unhealthy impulses transcending reason. So they tend to be directed to the sexual crimes, misconducts or violent crimes, or accompany mental disorders such as schizophrenia.

By the relative original power which is relative with the spirituality behind the personality, we determine our behaviors according to the motivation based on the exercise in the consciousness. So, the personality channel and the function and the ability of chakras are the important factor in determining the spiritual wave.

3-70 Culture and civilization based on spiritual dimension

According to the relative wave based on spiritual dimension, the entire consciousness will be directed by the "principle of dimensional integration," from the spiritual dimension of individual to family,

Chapter Three ☆ The Turning Point

clan, ethnic group, and nation.

The criterion of personality and spirituality are totally different between families, such as, one is involved with the spirituality of the higher spiritual dimension, and another is involved with the lower spiritual dimension. This makes their fate different.

Religious history is the important factor to determine the spiritual dimension of the ethnic group and the nation, and it has built the mental culture and guided human minds. The science civilization has achieved evolution relatively with the mental culture based on religious history, so if science technology had flourished in the era of poor spiritual dimension, it would definitely reach to destruction by war.

Whether it is the higher spiritual dimension or the lower spiritual dimension of the ethnic group and the nation, the formation history is based on their religious history, and it can be verified quite obviously from the cultural heritage whether they have built the highly scientific civilization and peaceful nation, or not.

It will make a significant difference for the mental culture and the science culture, based on spiritual evolution, whether the ethnic group and the nation legalize discrimination toward women openly such as polygamy and the caste system, or they restrict the status of women with the male logic in the center, such as monotheism, Hinduism, and Confucianism which favors the male domination over women, or they guarantee status and freedom for women and have built their culture and civilization.

There are two major methods to evaluate whether it is the higher spiritual dimension or the lower spiritual dimension for the ethnic group and nation; one is the improvement and development of the economic culture, and the other is the improvement and development of sexual differentiation.

The spiritual dimension of the nation and the personality level of the people of the nation in the spiritual evolution would be verified by releasing the amount of material desire and domination desire, the "instinctive remaining consciousness," which both have been derived from dietary desire and sexual desire, the "instinctive survival consciousnesses," So, it will be divided into two types of nations, whether the people of the nation are released from the dietary desire consciousness accompanied by economic improvement and development and can live a comfortable life in peace without hunger, or whether they suffer from poverty and hunger by the economic collapse.

For the benefit of the science civilization accompanied by spiritual evolution, scientific technology and economic development have gradually released us from the time axis domination and labor burden by physical domination, and directed us to freedom. Therefore, we must understand that the benefit from the science civilization is not the result of the improvement in intellectual ability, but is the result of the spiritual evolution based on the rule of "spirit is subjective and body is objective."

However, the think tank group who's thoughts based on the rule of "body is subjective and spirit is objective" has a strong desire for the science almighty principle, accelerating arrogant pride, and has caused various environmental problems such as natural destruction and global warming. The destruction of the nature which forms all harmony and order for the terrestrial lives accelerates the destruction of family environment and social

Chapter Three ☆ The Turning Point

environment without anyone noticing, and it continues to increase environmental destruction, so we human beings are now headed toward the destruction of the entire earth.

I can explain the fact that the delay of science technology and economic development proves the delay of spiritual evolution itself.

Sorrow and ONSHU of women in the triangle relationship caused by discrimination against women by the male type sexual desire dominating structure according to the "principle of physical dimensional domination" in the prison star, has become the core of ONSHU for the entire earth, and it is the key for the fate of the earth star in the future. When the countries which delayed their spiritual evolution because of the existence of discrimination against women, obtain the science technology to develop offensive weapons such as nuclear weapons, will eventually go to the extreme of suicide bombing by the theory of struggle and destruction. If so, the world will be forced to choose the path to Self-destruction.

Another important key is whether or not evolutionary sexual differentiation has been built. The ethnic and the national spiritual dimension will be determined by whether the nations form their social structures by dictatorial ways in which adultery and other unequal laws for divorce are legally executed, and gender discrimination is significant by the male type dominating structure, or they form the equal social structure of free and equal opportunity toward women. We can perceive the spiritual dimension by the spiritual evolution of ethnic groups and nations. A symbol of how closed the society is to women is how many women can advance to the congress as the legislative branch of government and the central government offices as administrative branch of government.

In the 21st century, we should live the way of life of PARAREVO and transform to the love pair system of SHINSEI unity, build the collaboration world which is the sphere type integration structure with women as the subject. It will be important whether we can change to the structure of equal opportunity without gender discrimination, and transform to the female type integration structure, from family to society, nation, and the world, according to the "principle of love dimensional integration" of women and men.

Since the largest core of discrimination in human history is the one against women, the social advancement for women will make the power of love, integration, and creation in the entire society and culture, and the civilization will improve and develop, rapidly. On the other hand, a person in the lower spiritual dimension with strong physical world benefits and material and sexual desires will descend again to the poor nation with inconvenience and severe labor by the feudal system under a dictatorship regime, and hold problems and assignments in the next world by his/her own cause, according to the "rule of reincarnation," based on the "rule of spiritual causality."

3-71. Energy waves in the 7 spiritual dimensions

The spiritual wave is determined by the dimension of the spirituality, the speed, and the qualitative energy, and exists in the "intangible substantial world" according to the spiritual dimension. The base of the qualitative energy of the material wave exists in the "Ether plane." It consists of three layer dimensional structures which are, the mineral wave, the plant wave, and the animal wave.

Chapter Three ☆ The Turning Point

Spiritual waves composed of spiritual dimensions of the four major layers, which are the "Astral plane," the ghost world wave, the "Mental plane," the spirit world wave, the "Causal plane," the "Enlightened Spirit world" wave, and the "Monad plane," the universal love sphere structure with the soul and SHINSEI, allow the generation and the development to be sustainable eternally as the SHINSEI integrated life entity. Those four spiritual waves and three "Ether planes" compose the seven layers of the spiritual dimensions.

It often happens that even if you seek and wish for something, good things are hard to Self-actualize. On the other hand, bad things come easily into reality. This is because the spiritual waves of the "Astral entity" in the lower dimension are easier to be relative with the personality level centered in the physical world benefits. Compared with the spiritual wave of the higher spiritual dimension in the "Causal plane," the spiritual wave of the lower dimension is easier to be relative with the physical world waves, so the relative original power based on the spirit and mind of the lower dimension is easy to derive and exercise. This is the reason bad and undesirable things, derived by uncomfortable feelings such as complaint and dissatisfaction, are easier to crystallize than the good things and lofty ideal wishes.

In order to be relative with the spirituality in the higher spiritual dimension, we should improve our own personality dimension with the great virtue of unselfishness by Self-sacrifice and release the chakras from the physical domination of the physical body, which will increase the spin speed of the chakras and the speed of the consciousness, raising to a higher dimension, and expand the size and capacity of the chakras to the cosmic dimension, based on the way of life of PARAREVO.

3-72. SHINSEI (true sense) is the common denominator of the entire universe

The whole creator world of the universe is forced to exist according to each spiritual dimension, by the relative original power which was created by the slight fluctuation of imperfection with SHINSEI, the "relative universal original power." So, SHINSEI exists relatively as the common denominator for the whole creator world in the universe.

Therefore, the spiritual life consciousness, which is the qualitative energy, contained in each creator world is systematized as a molecule. For example, ants make their life by SHINSEI, systematize the shape and the form as ants based on the consciousness form of the spiritual consciousness entity as ants, and manifest the individual mental entity as ants. And elephants make their life by SHINSEI, systematize the shape and the form as elephants based on the consciousness form of the spiritual consciousness entity as elephants, and manifest the individual mental entity as elephants. Also Human beings are alive by SHINSEI, systematize the shape and the form as human beings based on the consciousness form of the spiritual consciousness entity as human beings, and manifest the individual mental entity as human beings.

The spiritual life entities in the higher spiritual dimension in Buddhism and Christianity, such as Bodhisattva and angels existing in the higher spiritual dimension are alive by the relative original power with SHINSEI, manifest as systematized shape and form by each consciousness form, and exist in the spiritual world as the individual mental entity for completing each role and responsibility.

The verity of the individual entity, SHINSEI, is the common denominator of the whole creator world in the universe and comprehends the entire universe as SHINSEI integration consciousness world based on the SHINSEI unity, by systematizing the spiritual consciousness entity (each individual mental entity) as a molecule, and organically networking all to form harmony and order universally. If there is no SHINSEI as the common denominator in the universe, the entropy increases unlimitedly, expanding disharmony and disorder, and the universe itself will be destroyed.

All things in the whole creator world are referred to Self-determination based on the free intention of molecules (individual mental entities) with SHINSEI as the common denominator, and manifest according to the direction of Self-completion with the guarantee of Self-responsibility. This is the principle and fundamental rule that makes the universe free and equal.

The method to connect the relative wave with the higher spiritual dimension is to make Self-effort to go up the steps of the spiritual dimension, one by one.

People of the non-PARAREVO world make external criticism and evaluation according to the "principle of dimensional domination" by external separation. They easily blame another person, such as that person is bad, this person is wrong, and it is his fault, etc. They are looking at the external part based on the rule of "body is subjective and spirit is objective," and shift their responsibility to others by victim consciousness, and fall in to Self-injuriours behavior activity being dominated by uncomfortable feelings such as complaints and dissatisfaction, so, they are creating the demon's world inside their spirit and mind.

People of the PARAREVO world look inside themselves with eyes of the spiritual consciousness entity based on the rule of "spirit is subjective and body is objective," direct their consciousness to modesty and humility with the Self-examination and penitence of a wrongdoer consciousness as the life entity of the prison star, accept as they are unconditionally, with gratitude and joy, according to the "principle of dimensional integration" by internal separation between the "soul mind" and the "body mind" contained in themselves, and create peace and relief inside their spirit and mind, and release to freedom.

People in the poor spiritual dimension are not able to overcome their "body mind" with their "soul mind" by their narrow and base-mindedness. Those people always say that it is just an ideal theory and will never happen but the theory of PARAREVO is not asking the impossible, it is saying that *all things are directed to Self-determination, Self-responsibility, and Self-completion based on free intention.* So, it is totally up to the spiritual dimension of the person whether it is possible to live a way of PARAREVO, or not. And it is also a matter of integration and domination in the criterion of the "soul mind" and the "body mind" based on the truth, the *presence of the consciousness based on SHINSEI.*

All things are in conformity with the Self-determination based on free intention, and guarantee of Self-responsibility, and supported by the principle and the fundamental rule of Self-effort which directs to Self-Enlightenment and spiritual evolution.

3-73. The relative original power with the high-dimensional being

When you want to improve your personality, you will be able to do so by connecting with the relative original power of a person in the higher spiritual dimension. When you want to improve your spirituality, there is a fundamental principle and rule by which you can connect, by the relative wave, with a spiritual being in the higher spiritual dimension and direct to the spirituality formation of the higher dimension by the "rule of the relative original power" based on the spirit and mind.

Nowadays, unlike in the past, we have been given a favor by the science civilization. We are now able to interchange our sentiment by communicating with everybody at the real time, by mobile phone and other IT devices, anytime and anywhere. If you would like to communicate with someone by using a mobile phone, you need three things, a mobile phone itself, an address for access, and a provider to connect you to another person.

To connect the relative wave with a spiritual being in the higher spiritual dimension and spiritually interact with the spiritual wave, firstly we need a corresponding tool, something like a mobile phone. Since the common denominator for the life entity in the entire universe is SHINSEI, SHINSEI is like a mobile phone. It would be impossible for your spirit to communicate with the spiritual being in the higher dimension without coming face to face with SHINSEI, as SHINSEI joint entity. In doing so we must achieve the Self-discovery of the presence of SHINSEI and manifest it internally.

Secondly, we need some sort of address. Since each of us has proper name and address in order to identify ourselves, the spiritual being in the higher spiritual dimension also has proper logos and address, according to each spiritual dimension, and it will be possible to be relative by SHINGON, *the spirit which is present in words based on SHINSEI.* Because the meaning of the word SHINGON, SHIN meaning SHINSEI and GON meaning spirit of language, SHINGON is the logos as the address to connect the relative wave with SHINSEI as the common denominator. Even if you repeat a mantra as existing religions do, unless the presence of the spirit of language based on SHINSEI is systematized in you and manifested and made logos as SHINGON, it is impossible to connect the relative wave with a spiritual being in the higher spiritual dimension. In existing religions, when you only shout a mantra as the address, if you do not know the presence of SHINSEI as a mobile phone, you are only in the world of delusion, indulging in Self-satisfaction and Self-intoxication, and the mantra has become a dead letter. Therefore, invocation of Amida, Buddhist scriptures, and prayers which the religion world has devoted to the external God and Buddha, echo in vain and are meaningless. So, I would say that religions have invested a long religious history in momentary effort, and never interacted spiritually with the spiritual being in the higher spiritual dimension.

Thirdly, we should make a contract with the provider who can connect you to a spiritual being in the higher dimension. The provider is SHINSEI, the source of power which is the same root and the same origin with the whole creator world in the entire

Chapter Three ☆ The Turning Point

universe, and we should register a proper name and the address to the spiritual world, and connect the spiritual line at a place where the door to the spiritual world of the higher spiritual dimension is located, by SHINSEI integration consciousness. The place of the higher spiritual dimension is not the same with shrines and Buddhist temples of the poor and lower dimension, or mountain worship places where wishes for the excessive physical world benefits and selfishness are swirling and have accumulated things such as "we want this" or "please do that."

In order to register spiritually in the higher spiritual dimension, it is necessary to do both substantial work and spiritual work to connect the spiritual line to the higher spiritual dimension with SHINSEI as the common denominator. Payment method to the provider, SHINSEI of the universe, is to contribute to the larger entire purpose and to increase the acceptance degree of love and the freedom degree for the consciousness, according to *the great virtue of unselfishness by Self-sacrifice, release your own ONSHU by loving your ONSHU* based on the equation of spiritual evolution.

For achievement of Self-completion for the true spirituality formation, we should transcend physical domination by releasing excessive physical world benefits, releasing the "rule of reincarnation" by the "rule of spiritual causality," connecting the relative wave positively with a spiritual being in the higher spiritual dimension, according to the "principle of dimensional integration" by internal separation, in order to graduate from the earth star, and to create the relative original power based on the spirit and mind, to exercise the consciousness based on love of SHINSEI, and to manifest the feelings of joy as the individual art of the higher dimension and open the door for Self-Enlightenment and spiritual evolution.

3-74. Unpleasant feelings are caused by spiritual disorder

In order to graduate from the earth star, we should complete the role and the responsibility of the individual purpose toward the entire purpose, and return the practice of love and the creation of joy to the earth star. However, the reason we are not able to make Self-completion, no matter how hard we try the practice of love and the creation of joy is because we are forced to exist in the relativity of the three layer structures, which is the triangle system of the physical relative materials and the relative wave based on SHINSEI.

We are unable, in our life, to avoid the influence of the spiritual wave from various spiritual dimensions and receive it unconsciously. When we go someplace, or enter a house or meet people, etc. carelessly, we invite unexpected situations because the spiritual waves arbitrarily invade beyond our consciousness.

Sometimes in our life, we fall into unpleasant feelings, suddenly, without knowing the reason. It is because we are receiving the spiritual waves of the lower dimension and being dominated by feelings such as dissatisfaction, jealousy, anger, and fear, etc., which might cause mental disorders such as depression and panic disorder. In some rare cases, a typical victim of an intense mental disorder, such as schizophrenia, anorexia and bulimia, would fall victim to Self-injurious behavior such as wrist cutting, withdrawal, behavior disorder, hysteria, etc. Auditory hallucination and illusion

Chapter Three ☆ The Turning Point

are the result of typical victim consciousness. During adolescence, triggered by a small incident, undifferentiated sexual desire consciousness and Kundalini syndrome are provoked and fall into spiritual disorder by destroying the "Sahasrara chakra" without the awareness of the adolescent, by the relative original power based on the evil spirit.

Since we are relative with all things all the time, physical illnesses appear by the same mechanism and system, so it is important for us to separate good things, bad things, and things not important in our life. In order to do so, we must cut the relative wave of the lower dimension, surround ourselves with a spiritual barrier, and make Self-effort to connect the spiritual wave and the relative wave of the higher dimension. Then it will be possible for us to create the relative original power of high quality love. For example, it will become possible to create miraculous power by facing the relative wave in the higher spiritual dimension with SHINSEI, connecting with chakras and logos, and creating SHINSEI integration consciousness by the relative original power of the trinity.

It is important to realize that Bodhisattvas in Buddhism and angels in Christianity also have a reason to be forced to be involved in the prison star, and we must understand that they have cause, problem, and assignment for being involved in the earth star. This means that they also have to graduate from the earth star by accomplishing spiritual evolution on their own. Based on the "rule of the universe," since the relative universal original power, SHINSEI, always directs to higher spiritual evolution, there is no other role or responsibility or reason to be involved. Even if they have no physical body, they must invoke the consciousness of, and work with the people in this world who are in a higher personality dimension, according to the "rule of the relative original power." And while doing so, they will achieve Self-completion with the contribution of love and creation of joy and climb up the steps in their spiritual dimension for the great cause called the entire purpose.

In doing this, we create higher motivation constantly by improving the truth based on the spiritual dimension of our own self, straining the spiritual barrier to cut the relative waves from the poor spiritual dimension in the lower dimension, and protecting the spiritual line to connect the spirit. To avoid the condition that would cause our consciousness not to fall in to unpleasant feelings by being persuaded by the spiritual waves in the lower dimension, we should not empathize by being relative with persons and materials in the lower spiritual dimension. By cutting the spiritual waves, the spiritual disorders will be solved rapidly and the conditions will be improved.

The method for this is to try hard to draw the separation boundary line between oneself and others in order not to direct to shifting responsibility by victim consciousness according to the "principle of dimensional domination" by external separation. Also it is important to learn the method to cut the spiritual waves in the lower dimension, which come to be relative unilaterally, and protect the spiritual line of the spirit from the waves of the dogma of evil spirits.

3-75. The way of life to integrate individual purpose and entire purpose

In order to direct the individual purpose to the entire purpose of the higher dimension and integrate the consciousness to the higher spiritual dimension to graduate from the earth star, we must achieve Self-management by Self-determination based on the "rule of freedom" and Self-completion of the role and the responsibility for the existing purpose according to Self-responsibility. By doing this, we will be able, for the first time, to achieve the practice of love and the creation of joy toward others and to contribute toward the entire purpose.

So, instead of depending on organizations, groups, the nation, or anything else, we should exercise the way of life of PARAREVO, which releases *the "principle of dependence and domination"* in order to obtain true freedom and bear Self-responsibility for all things, according to *the "principle of independence and freedom."* That means we should reform theoretical frameworks and values of religious theory and philosophical theory, which are theories based on lies and untruths, and achieve Self-completion to the higher spiritual dimension to direct to Self-Enlightenment and spiritual evolution.

It is important to suggest the real purpose for life to many people, and awaken them to the spiritual evolution, from values of mere physical world benefits, and direct them to *the "principle of independence and freedom"* for release from physical domination and acquisition of freedom.

3-76. Create the path to manifest SHINSEI (true sense)

Some people might say that the theory of PARAREVO is *understood clearly but hard to do.* This is because we have *the habit of the mind and the soul,* which has been tamed by inconvenience and desire throughout 3.8 billion years, in the physical dominating structure by the "instinctive survival consciousnesses." If you live your life for just living, thinking only for the present, and keeping your existing purpose and value at the earth level, the spiritual consciousness entity would be held in inconvenience and desire even after disembodiment, moving instantly back to the "intangible substantial world" of the earth star, and would repeat the tangible and the intangible life entity of the earth dimension, again and again, holding the obsession of this world and ONSHU, according to the "rule of reincarnation."

Rarely do I hear people say, "it's not entirely bad living on the earth star," which I think is a lower level spiritual dimension idea. Most of the people who are saying this are arrogant and reign at the top of the food chain, thinking in the dominating range. Those people are not able to understand another person's pain, because they worship the physical world benefits and having arrogance and conceit inside the consciousness, they do not hear the scream of animals and plants in the natural world and the heartrending cry of the whole creator world. They do not know that they will be charged for their unawareness, by the whole creator world, when they go to the spiritual world. In the spiritual world, they will finally realize that *ignorance is a "shade of death," and does not produce any true emotion, which means they are only living for the*

Chapter Three ☆ The Turning Point

sake of living however they are not really living, they are dead.

So, what is *the "rule of SHINSEI manifestation?"* It is the life you live when you have courage to part from the desire consciousness of the excessive physical world benefits and choose to live with the great virtue of unselfishness by Self-sacrifice. When we are given trial, sadness, and suffering such as cancer and intractable disease, we are able to face ourselves for the first time, and ask why this did happen to me? So, you must transcend resentment by love, release the resentment ("body mind") contained in you, and open the path to spiritual evolution. The theory of PARAREVO suggests that trials and sufferings become the reverse power and energy for dimensional conversion to the higher spiritual dimension, and *creates the path to "SHINSEI manifestation"* where the inner SHINSEI (the SHINSEI that makes you really alive) resides. It is impossible to manifest SHINSEI unless we fully realize the ugliness of the earth star and lowness of the spiritual dimension and feel pain from our innermost feeling toward the existence of the body, and decide not to bear the physical body again.

As long as we human beings think that the earth is not so bad while we are reining at the top of the food chain and slaughtering and exploiting all kinds of lives without any repentance, we are in too low a level of the spiritual dimension. And we are a long way from graduating from the earth, and will repeat reincarnation many times.

The persons who are blessed by the physical world benefits and devoted to vested interests and wealthy living, have a stronger obsession and more difficult assignments in this world. However, a far more serious thing for those people is that there are too many conditions to be charged by the whole creator world, so it is very hard to graduate from the earth, and they will have to stay in the ugly and poor spiritual world for a long time. People who have many material possessions become dominant and bring inconvenience to the creator world, so they have created, inside themselves, the world of inconvenience and desire, which is totally opposite from the world of freedom and love. It means they will go to the world of inconvenience and desire by themselves, and go to the ugly and poor spiritual world where only similar people stay, and continue to be charged by the whole creator world. This is the reason for the saying "it is more difficult for rich people to enter heaven than it is for a camel to pass through the eye of needle" or "how blessed poor people are because heaven is in the palm of their hands."

The purpose of life is to prepare for the spiritual life. That is, we prepare the spiritual world, every day, where we will go, and our consciousness and actions become the memories of the soul. "Hell" or the Devil's world is not created by the King of Hell or devils. The consciousness world is the world which you created by yourself, by Self-determination and Self-management and Self-completion by Self-responsibility based on the free intention of yourself. When you exercise the "body mind," you prepare your "Hell" world by yourself, and when you exercise the "soul mind," you prepare your "Heaven" by yourself.

The "rule of reincarnation" is led by Self-determination and Self-responsibility and we all bear the role and the responsibility for Self-completion.

Everything grows well in severe environment, but blessed and well-ordered environment only raises poor persons. This relates to all things in common. History has already and clearly proven that it is impossible to find SHINSEI in the social structure, religions, the mental world, and even less success in philosophy and psychology, which only seek the physical world benefits. It is because, basically, the direction of seeking SHINSEI is totally different.

We only see the trees but cannot see the forest. Like ants, which do not care about the existence of Mt. Fuji and end their life by being preoccupied with immediate things, human beings do the same. We do not care about the universe even though it exists as an undeniable fact, and end our life by being preoccupied with immediate things, just like ants. When we discuss things about the earth while we are on the earth, we cannot understand anything about the earth, and we are not able to find any answers about this world while we are in this world. The existing purpose in this world is to prepare for the spiritual world, so actually the true purpose for life exists beyond death.

The PARAREVO theory suggests a clear vision and paradigm for graduation from the earth, so we will never have to return to the earth again.

3-77. Advent of "the Eschatology" in Christianity and "the declining days of this world" in Buddhism

The content I am going to explain here is the important message in the "sacred revelation from the universe," as the Cosmic Bible, and is a completely original idea from PARAREVO. It will be a core prophecy and proposal for the earth and human beings which are the destiny and the direction to take in the future. The theoretical framework and the paradigm of value of this "revelation," based on the "cosmological evidence," will definitely be the sacred revelation to be handed down from generation to generation forever, in the coming human history.

As I mentioned in my previous book "PARADIGM REVOLUTION," the earth is being invaded by the macro threat called nuclear mass destruction weapons, and micro threats such as cancer cells, AIDS, Ebola hemorrhagic fever, and new viruses. Even during the era of Buddha and Jesus Christ, there was no such crisis in which the earth star itself was destroyed and all life entities on the earth were annihilated. However, by verifying various phenomena happening on the earth in this era and comparing them with objective facts, it is no exaggeration to say that we are now in the era, which Christianity and Buddhism predicted as "the Eschatology" and "the declining days of this world."

The termination ideology is the thought based on the historical view that *there is an end to our history, and it is the purpose of history itself* as proposed by monotheism such as Judaism, Christianity, and Islam. The ideology of the decline of Buddhism is *the historical view with the death of Buddha as the starting point and the thought based on the historical view that after the death of Buddha, the Buddhist laws, which are the teachings of Siddhartha Gautama, would decline by the three steps from Age of the True Dharma to Age of the Semblance Dharma and Age of the Final Dharma together with the history, and the teachings of Buddha would gradually collapse and no longer be valid.*

Why is now the era of the termination or the era of the decline of Buddhism? I would like to discuss two thoughts based on *the true*

Chapter Three ☆ The Turning Point

messages from the universe.

In order for us to understand the background of the era, it is important to verify the *era of the present* based on religious historical view, and grasp the worldview, because the religious historical views are the facts by which religions have built the foundations of the cultural environment and led the history. There are various cultural areas in the world such as Judaism cultural area, Islamic cultural area, Christian cultural area, Buddhist cultural area, Hindu cultural area, Confucius cultural area, etc. Politics have been governed by religious authorities and all sorts of things have been shaped based on this fact. As proof, even though all other buildings have disappeared, still remaining today are the clay figures, earthenware figures, ancient tombs, ruins, shrines and temples as "the fingerprint of our history." As we can see from this, religion was always in the center of the culture. Religious theoretical frameworks and values have given mental education and become the votive light, formed the social framework, formed the ethnic groups, and formed the civilization together with the culture of each nation.

The culture and the civilization have achieved evolution and development by working together, so without mental evolution the material civilization would not have developed. Had nuclear bombs existed in the savage era in which people cruelly murdered even their parents or brothers in the struggle for supremacy like the Crusades or the Warring States period, they would have used it as if it were nothing but a tool for the strengthening of their own power, and if so, it is easy to see that the earth star would have already fallen into destruction at that point and became the debris planet with no presence of life at all.

You might think that human beings would not do such stupid things; however, human beings are stupid animals. As proof, there is an undeniable historical fact that only 70 years ago, during World War second, the United States dropped an atomic bomb on Hiroshima and another on Nagasaki without any analysis or verification of such tragic results. This fact itself has proven the savagery and stupidity of human beings, more than anything else. The United States has never made any apology for dropping the atomic bombs, repeating the nuclear tests over and over again for nuclear development to justify nuclear bombs. Even now, the US is placed in the central position as the world`s number one nuclear possession country, but nuclear disarmament action has gone very slow and made very little progress.

Throughout numerous histories, we have repeated struggles and wars over and over because of the differences in cultural theoretical framework and values. Still now, it is reality that there are problems in the Middle East such as the extension war of the Crusades between Christianity and Islam.

3-78. "The Eschatology" in Christianity and "the declining days of this world" in Buddhism, based on the view of religious history

I am going to verify the current background of this era based on the view of religious history, and will tell *the sacred revelation from the universe.* So I would like to refer to the mathematical historical view in the Old Testament and the New Testament regarding "the

Chapter Three ☆ The Turning Point

Eschatology," which is the historical view of monotheism such as Judaism, Christianity, and Islam. It is because the global historical view at the present time is all standardized with BC and AD by the Western calendar.

The historical view of the Old Testament started from Genesis with the base of Adam and Eve who were said to be the ancestors of human beings. Abraham has been worshiped and revered as a saint and the father of faith by both of the two main religions, Christianity and Islam, which have had confrontations because of the differences in their view of God. There are more than 3 billion religious people in the world who are believers in Abraham.

The 2,000 year period from the birth of Adam and Eve to the birth of Abraham and Sarah, is in the first stage of the historical view based on the belief of God. The next 2,000 year period from Abraham and Sarah to Jesus, the founder of Christianity, and Mary Magdalene is in the second stage of the historical view based on the belief of God in the Old Testament. That 4,000-year history has flowed together with those two historical views. After the death of Jesus, who was considered the Messiah, the 2,000-year historical view based on Christianity has been established and continues to the present time. That is, the starting point of Adam and Eve, from the Old Testament, and combined with the New Testament, the 6,000 years of history has passed, and every 2,000 years saints were born.

The monotheistic view of history is that there will be an end to our history and that is the purpose of the history itself. They believe stubbornly that the end of the world will come by a convulsion of nature, which is dependent on other facts. They call this Armageddon (the end of the world), however, they haven't mentioned exactly when.

Because of the fact that mitochondrial is only inherited from the mother, we can trace the maternal ancestors by the mutation analysis method. The origin of human beings is in the woman called mitochondrial Eve, in Africa, approximately 160,000 years ago. Modern humans were born in Africa expanding the habitat to Asia and Europe through the Middle East, and then, after becoming a contiguous continent by the climate change, such as the Ice Age, expanded to North America and South America. *About 6,000 years ago, agriculture had begun in various areas in the world simultaneously, and at the same time, civilization occurred and the foundation of modern humans was established.* From this fact, the content of the Old Testament mentioned 6,000 years ago, seemed to fit the human embryology.

The ideology of the decline of Buddhism says that *after the death of Buddha, the Buddhist laws which are the teachings of Siddhartha Gautama would decline in three steps from the Age of the True Dharma to the Age of the Semblance Dharma, and the Age of the Final Dharma together with the history, but 56.7 million years later, Mirokubosatsu (Maitreya) who will finish ascetic practices in the Tusita Heaven will come back as advent Buddha or future Buddha (Tathagata) and save mankind.* Japanese religious founders had preached the idea of salvation by positioning each era as the age of the Final Dharma, and had submitted the new religions actively to the public.

However, there was no atomic bomb in their era, unlike the present time, so it was hard to say that era was not the age of the

Final Dharma (the end of the earth). It was a vulgar and easy idea of salvation which manifested *the "principle of dependence and domination."* They replaced the people's poverty and hunger as if it was the age of the Final Dharma, used their supposition and made delusion and illusion of going to the land of Perfect Bliss if people prayed to Buddha, repeated sutra.

3-79. The sacred revelation from the universe

The "sacred revelation from the universe" says that *the time of "the Eschatology" in Christianity and "the declining days of this world" in Buddhism, has come.* The message from this revelation has the important meaning and significance for the present day, because as I explained earlier the time of 6,000 years has passed through the three stages.

A symbolic phenomenon, the "September 11 attacks," happened immediately after the very beginning of the 21 century. Islamic fundamentalist terrorists attacked the Twin Towers of the World Trade Center in New York. What does this phenomenon mean and suggest to us?

In 1991, the Union of Soviet Socialist Republics, which was the symbol of communism, collapsed, so that the era of the Cold War ended and closed the curtain of ideological struggle. 10 years later, the two buildings in the US, which were the symbol of the Jewish wealth of Rothschild and Rockefeller and also the symbol of American capitalism, collapsed. This fact symbolizes the end of capitalism and at the same time, it suggests that the friction axis was shifted from the conflict of the ideology between socialism and capitalism to the religious conflict axis between Islam and Christianity, so that we entered the era of religious struggle.

In Buddhist scriptures, according to "the declining days of the world" ideology, it is said that 5.67 billion years after Buddha's death, Maitreya would appear again in this world and save mankind. However, the sacred message from the universe suggests that it was not the number of yeas but when the number of human beings increased to 5.67 billion population on the earth star, after the death of Buddha. The Cosmic Bible also suggests that the number 5.67 billion was switched from people to nonsensical years in order to keep many phony people from gaining power when the real age of the Final Dharma comes. So the true meaning was hidden.

The world population in the Old Testament of Adam and Eve's era, 6,000 years ago, was only 6 million. The world population in the era of Buddha was only about 60 million. In the age of Buddha, there was no world map, and nobody understood the earth was moving or the size of the earth or even the variety of races. In the worldview which was very narrow and a small population, the number of 5.67 billion people in the world would sound like a cosmological number and even more nonsensical. Moreover, if the "rule of reincarnation" based on the Buddhism theory is the universal truth, the rule would repeat eternally, so the population should be constant, a fixed number. The criterion of the time axis of one year of that time might have more credibility as 5.67 billion years than 5.67 billion people.

2,300 years after the death of Buddha, in the year 1,700, the number of human beings had reached 6 hundred million, which was 10 times more than the population in the Buddha's era. And

Chapter Three ☆ The Turning Point

in 1945 in Hiroshima, Pandora's box was opened for the first time, and the second time was in Nagasaki in the same year, which was dropping the atomic bombs and ending World War two. After 1945, we had the baby boomers and, we had experienced the largest global increase in population. It had never reached that number in human history.

Indeed, we human beings are at the top of the food chain on the earth star and kill all kinds of life and eat them, and exploit creation as we want. Human beings are greedy and egoistic and continue to destroy the ecological system, as if we are the cancer cells of the earth star. The world population reached 5.67 billion in 1995, occurring like cancer cells which propagated abnormally and progressed to the last stage.

In the year 1995, the Islamic world opened Pandora's box by developing an atomic bomb to be used against the Christian world. And that year happened to be the 50 year anniversary of the atomic bomb dropping on Hiroshima and Nagasaki. What does this mean? It suggests that nuclear weapons are diffused to the world of Christianity, Socialism, Hinduism, and Islam, and are possessed by dictatorships such as North Korea. The explosive worldwide crisis is expanded and now the collapse of the earth is manifested as reality.

In October 1996, there was big and shocking news not only for monotheism such as Christianity, Judaism, and Islam, but also for all religions in the world. It was the announcement by Pope John Paul II that he had acknowledged the theory of evolution. It was an epoch-making event when religions bowed to science for the first time, and accepted it as "the Day of Infamy" in religious history.

In the year 2000, the world population became a thousand times that of 6,000 years ago, increased by 100 times from the era of Buddha, and reached 6 billion people which is 10 times more than the year 1700, just 300 years ago.

The life entity on the earth began with a bacterium which was only single cell, as I explained earlier, and the cells of human beings have increased up to 60 trillion through 3.8 billion years. The number of cells is also meaningful. Six is the number of devil, so I would like to mention here that we enter the era to overcome the number of 6 by exceeding the macro population over 6 billion people.

Through 6,000 years of Jewish and Christian history, human population has reached 6 billion, and now is the era that the macro threat of atomic bombs could be diffused indiscriminately by foolish cancer cells called human being. Using the earth as a metaphor for one life entity, I must say, based on the sacred revelation from the universe, that every single existing thing goes to the fate of collapse, like the collapse of family, environment, the natural world, social order, the world economy, etc. The earth itself comes to serious illness like a terminally ill patient of cancer approaches the final hour, when the population reaches 5.67 billion human beings.

The nuclear weapon, atomic bomb, is converted into phenomenal thermal energy when radioisotopes increase and reach the critical point for fission, and immediately a chain reaction takes place. A similar phenomenon happens in cancer. The cancer cells increase with disorder and will become terminal cancer from advanced cancer when the cancer cells increase and reach the critical point for the entire cancer to fission, and immediately the chain reaction happens.

Both the threat of the atomic bomb and the threat of cancer are similar and use exactly the same mechanism, when it reaches to *the critical point for fission* by increasing the threat with disorder, which happens by some kind of triggering factors and it is the threatening collapse system which directs to destruction of the whole. When fission of atom, fission of cell, and fission of population become the actual threat, in the macro world fission of atom would be the nuclear weapons, and in the micro world fission of cell would be the cancer cell for the threat of each human being.

3-80. Human beings are the cancer cells of the terrestrial life entities

We human beings had achieved endless evolution and development in order to reign over the top of the food chain on the earth when we obtained desire and knowledge of the earth as a tool, but not love and wisdom of the universe. This fact proves, paradoxically, that *the human being is the most greedy, egoistic and dangerous creature among the terrestrial life.*

We also can't deny the fact that human beings have arrogantly ruined tens of millions of biological species co-existing on the earth and continue to destroy the global environment markedly by strengthening all kinds of desire supremacy principle and evil competition principle such as economic supremacy principle, academic supremacy principle, and scientific almighty principle. There are endless lists of what we have done to the earth, such as the environmental destruction with air and water pollution by industrial exhaust and liquid waste, also, global warming and desertification due to greenhouse gas such as carbon dioxide, and logging resulting in deforestation.

Since human beings are the greediest and most dangerous creatures among the terrestrial life, we are not able to make co-existence, co-prosperity, and symbiosis. Because of the insatiable desire of human egotism, we might hear the heartrending cry of Gaia, the terrestrial life entity. We as human beings must be aware of the fact that our physical environment is the epitome of the global environment and the destruction of the global environment destroys our physical environment. Our desires have dictated our evolution. Now we must recognize the fact that *human beings are the cancer cell of the terrestrial life entities (Gaia),* so we should take our responsibility seriously, since we are standing at the top of the food chain.

At the same time, we should also realize the fact that the real threat to human beings in the future is not *an external cause such as nuclear war or outside threat of bacillus such as virus.* The real threat is *the internal cause factor which are cancer cells caused by the nature of each person.* The ratio of the onset of cancer patients shows clearly that it has continued to grow at an ever-increasingly rate, yearly, and tends to increase rapidly now. As long as we human beings continue to direct our eyes and ears to the outside, there is no true awakening of the soul.

The fact that after 1995, human beings started abnormal multiplication, like cancer cells of the earth star, suggests that the abnormal multiplication of cancer cells inside the human body also started. The basic concept of the PARAREVO theory, the *individual*

Chapter Three ☆ The Turning Point

is the whole and the whole is the individual, is becoming common.

Religions, philosophies, and ideologies can't solve this problem. Moreover, it is impossible to do by international politics, the United Nations, or organizations such as W.H.O. It doesn't matter whether we have the status, reputation, or property, because this is the problem of our spiritual evolution and Self-Enlightenment in the spiritual dimension based on the personality (mind) and the spirituality (soul) of each person, and is why the universe made arrangements that illness of internal factors such as cancer and intractable diseases would spread all over the world in the declining era. It is for human beings to be directed to the true common existing purpose and the existing value by directing our eyes and ears to the mind and the soul.

The Cosmic Bible, the "sacred revelation from the universe," also states that if human beings are not able to complete spiritual evolution to the next dimension, the population will decrease to approximately 6 million by cancer and intractable diseases, like the populations we had 6,000 years ago.

It was 6 million years ago that human beings evolved into Homo Sapiens, and the world population which was 6 million in the era of Adam and Eve and 60 million in the era of Buddha reached to 6 billion in 2,000 AD, which was a thousand times that of Adam and Eve's era, and a hundred times that of Buddha's era, through the religious history of 6,000 years. Also, our body began from a primitive life entity of bacteria with only one cell and multiplied up to 60 trillion cells through 3.8 billion years.

You might have already noticed that *the number 6, the spirit number of the demon world* completed the age of termination. So, when *the number 6 is transcended by the number 7, which is the fortune number of the True spirit world,* it will be completed.

The PARAREVO theory considers that the spirit behind each number has a significant meaning. On August 27, 2007, 12 years after the year 1995, which was the year of the beginning of the *true termination period,* and 7 years after the year 2000, was the year when the population of human beings reached 6.6 billion, the universe gave the sacred word to the earth star. The sacred word from the universe was not like a savior or Messiah, but it came to the soul of each person as the cosmic truth based on the cosmological evidence. Now we are welcoming the time when all kinds of earth logical paradigm, which were considered good, such as existing theoretical frameworks and values of religious theory, ideology, economy, etc., would fade away and disappear on a global scale. From now on, common sense and established theories based on the earth logical evidence will be completely overthrown by this Cosmic Bible. The Cosmic Bible has *paradoxical theory and value* which is totally opposite of earth logical paradigm (paradoxical truth), based on the cosmological evidence.

Therefore, *the Cosmic Bible is not the Bible of the people on the earth, by the people on the earth, and for the people on the earth, but it is the Bible to complete the spiritual evolution to the spiritual dimension of the cosmic being, as the cosmic being, and for the cosmic being.*

We need the new cosmic truth in the era of termination. There is only one way for the world to be united beyond the nations, without intention and selfishness of each country. The world needs to have the common crises consciousness and the purpose to solve

Chapter Three ☆ The Turning Point

the threat of nuclear mass destruction weapons. And in order to do so, we should release all kinds of theoretical framework and values and reform radically, and unite with the common purpose consciousness, to avoid the crises.

3-81. The relative wave and the relative original power based on mind and spirit

Since all things in the universe are possible to exist according to *the relative wave in the spiritual dimension, and the "rule of the relative original power,"* the relative original power based on mind and spirit is created and makes the behavior based on the motivation by connecting the spiritual wave and the mental wave in the spiritual dimension with the relative wave in each dimension. I would like to explain in more detail about the relative wave based on mind and spirit and the "rule of the relative original power."

In mind and spirit, *mind is the personality consciousness entity which is formed by your own self in this world, based on your personality formation history, and spirit is the spirituality consciousness entity which was formed by your own self in your past life, based on your spiritual formation history.* So, the bad spirit world called the devil world or the good sprit world called heaven, religiously speaking, is the spiritual world which is created by your own self, and is not guided by some kinds of external factors or causes such as an ancestor's spirit or a vengeful spirit. Since the existing purpose and value of your life is only to prepare for the spiritual life, you go to the spiritual world, such as the evil spirit world or the good spirit world, after your death, which has been created by yourself, according to Self-management by Self-determination and Self-completion by Self-responsibility, based on the "rule of freedom."

According to the "rule of entropy relativity," the "soul mind" and the "body mind" exist in a slight fluctuation of imperfection based on SHINSEI, and are directed to opposite consciousness directions and forced to exist. Our truth is directed by the exercise of the consciousness based on SHINSEI, and is led to Self-determination based on the "rule of freedom" and whether we exercise the consciousness by the relative original power between the "soul mind" and SHINSEI or by the "body mind" and SHINSEI, and it will be Self-completed by your Self-responsibility.

When you invoke many unpleasant feelings by the relative original power between SHINSEI and the "body mind," you end up creating an evil spirit world inside yourself unconsciously, direct yourself to Self-hatred and Self-denial, and invite Self-injurious behavior such as illness of unknown origin or unexpected accident by the devil world you created inside yourself, you will create Self-destruction in your spiritual world and in the real world. When you invoke many feelings of gratitude and joy by the relative original power between SHINSEI and the "soul mind," you create a good spirit world inside yourself, unconsciously, being directed to Self-affection and Self-affirmation by the creativity of free love of yourself, and Self-create to Self-Enlightenment and spiritual evolution by inviting the chain of happiness.

Therefore, we should understand that, by the "rule of preservation by inscription," our personality creates new spirituality, and the evil spirit world and the good spirit world are the spiritual world

Chapter Three ☆ The Turning Point

that we create instantaneously in this world by ourselves. Since we are forced to exist in this world by the three-layer structure of the triangle system between SHINSEI, the "soul mind" and the "body mind," it is important to understand the nature of the "soul mind" and the "body mind."

Since SHINSEI is contained in all things, and it is *the true sense* which is possible to be relative according to each spiritual dimension, and is the core to produce the relative original power, the "soul mind" and the "body mind" are able to exist in the slight fluctuation of imperfection. The "soul mind" is directed to the creation of the individual art of joy based on free love, according to the rule of "spirit is subjective and body is objective," and the "body mind" is directed to the desire of physical domination and the physical world benefits by the instinctive survival consciousnesses based on inconvenient ONSHU, according to the rule of "body is subjective and spirit is objective."

So, *the "soul mind" is the intention that the soul, the spiritual consciousness entity, directs, and the "body mind" is the intention that the physical desire directs.* The three-layer structure by the triangle system between SHINSEI, the spiritual consciousness entity, and the physical body raise all kinds of problems and make things complicated.

Life entity in the higher spiritual dimension in the universe creates the sustainable relative original power, based on the sphere theory of the two layers, by the pair system of SHINSEI and the spiritual consciousness entity, and exists by the mechanism which makes possible eternal generation and development. The spiritual life entity which is able to exist eternally by this mechanism is called *"SHINSEI integrated life entity."*

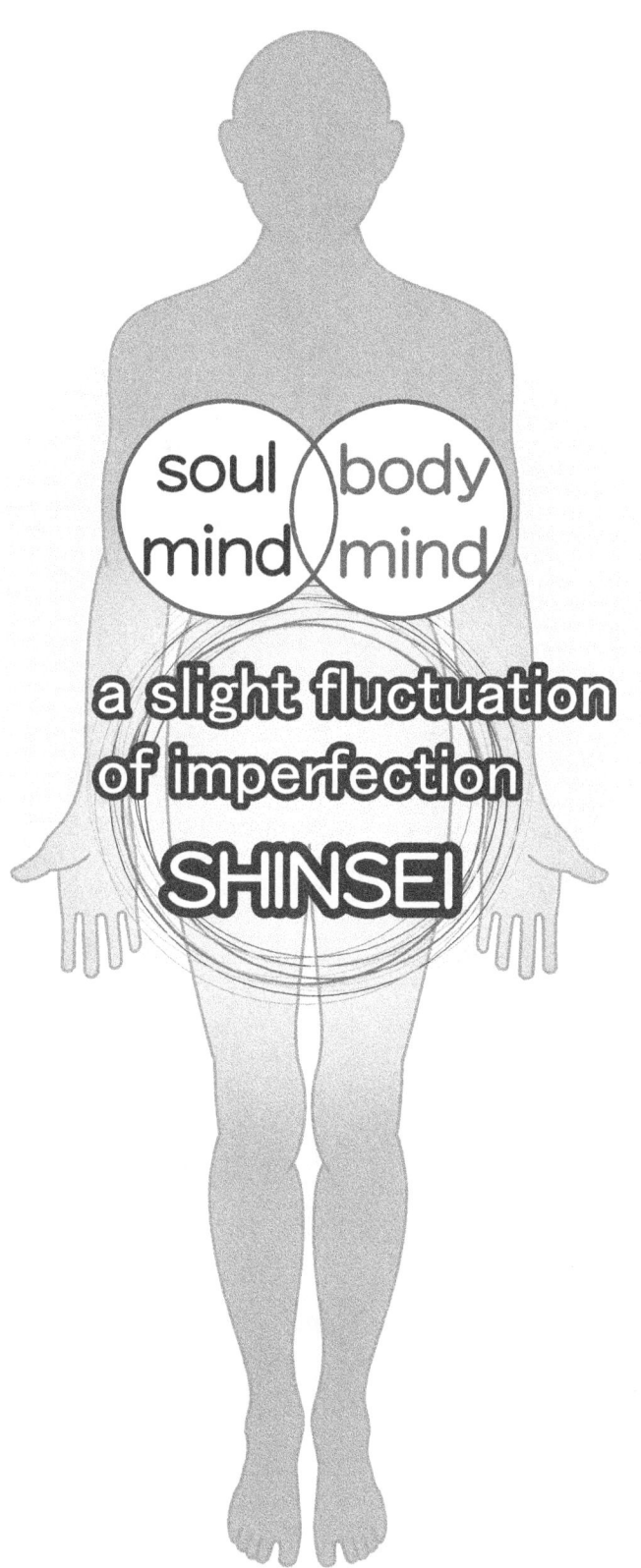

Contents for Book 4 : Chapter Four ☆ The Conclusion

4-1. Definition of truth and fact in the PARAREVO theory
4-2. There is no fact better than truth
4-3. Internal nature of truth and external nature of fact
4-4. External separation of fact and internal separation of truth
4-5. Self-integration of truth and Self-domination of fact
4-6. "Thought of remorse" of truth and "thought of grudge" of fact
4-7. Verification of the way of life of Jesus and the way of life of PARAREVO
4-8. Logos for the way of life of PARAREVO
4-9. Truth is in now and fact is in time axis
4-10. Life is with Self-determination and Self-responsibility
4-11. Universe is undeniable existentialism
4-12. The secret of truth to live in the now
4-13. The rule of "spirit is subjective and body is objective" will release the genetic linkage
4-14. The PARAREVO theory shows the "rule of the attainment of speritual being during life"
4-15. The "rule of genetic linkage" will lead to unhealthy dependence and shift responsibility to others
4-16. Self-integration in the thought of child and parents
4-17. The now will release causality under the time axis
4-18. Life is based on the rule of Self-responsibility
4-19. Addiction to religion is similar to schizophrenia
4-20. Flashback phenomena of consciousness of past lives
4-21. Emerging consciousness is the final chapter of spiritual evolution
4-22. View of life in the universe and on the earth is paradoxical theory and rule
4-23. The mechanism of birth of lives born on the earth
4-24. The Relative relationship between the physical body and the soul
4-25. The "rule of causality" and the "rule of karma" will collapse
4-26. Spiritual evolution and the "exclusion theory by jealousy" are opposite
4-27. Logos to release emerging consciousness
4-28. Logos to live in the now
4-29. Separation of "I" is the true way of life
4-30. Separation borderline between love and kindness

4-31. Only truth exists in the spiritual world
4-32. Lose truth being fooled by fact
4-33. Separation borderline between self and others in the personality formation history
4-34. Time to face the natural world seriously
4-35. The time for judgment by water
4-36. Now is the time to receive judgment from water
4-37. Separation borderlines between oneself and others in the material world
4-38. Truth of separation borderline between oneself and others and the natural environment
4-39. The social environment and the personality formation history based on the view of values
4-40. Outer evaluation as fact and inner evaluation as truth
4-41. The foundation of the Constitution is established by religions
4-42. The 20th century was the era of ideological strife
4-43. The 21st century is the era of religious strife
4-44. The 21st century is the era to release from religious spell
4-45. Religion exists in our individual truth
4-46. Religious dependence and shifting responsibility by victim consciousness
4-47. Religious dependence and chain of unhappiness
4-48. The vertical and horizontal personality formation history
4-49. Prenatal environment and the ground environment of saints are paradox
4-50. Habit of mind is inherited from mother
4-51. Roles and responsibilities of a couple with ideal love
4-52. Material wealth produces poor mind
4-53. Separation borderline between self and others and true spiritual relationship of parent-child
4-54. Marital relationship is the second ONSHU
4-55. A pair system of love and the relative original power
4-56. The four rules of relativity based on the spiritual dimension
4-57. The historical perspective of legalized male dominating structure
4-58. Love of women and men is the height of "the relative art"
4-59. The time axis is like a virtual world
4-60. Evolution is the way to release from the time axis domination
4-61. Women who are in the high-spiritual dimension are the driving force of evolution

4-62. The way of life of PARAREVO transcends the time-axis
4-63. Spiritual consciousness and physical consciousness are paradox
4-64. The principal of dimensional integration of the cosmological love
4-65. Establish Self-integrity by the way of PARAREVO life
4-66. SHINSEI is the receptor for everything in the universe
4-67. SHINSEI is the receptor for everything of the entire personality
4-68. The importance of Logos and the concept of way of life
4-69. All necessary things have to be good
4-70. True Self-realization is unconditional Self-completion
4-71. The way of PARAREVO life makes your entire life "lucky"
4-72. The "rule of freedom" is the fundamental rule of the universe
4-73. SHINSEI itself evolves by the "rule of freedom"
4-74. The 21st century is the end of monotheism
4-75. The "rule of freedom" based on Self-responsibility
4-76. The "rule of the relative field" based on love
4-77. Individual mental entities manifest individual art
4-78. Individual subjectivity makes individual arts sustainable
4-79. Individual subjectivity releases the past practice of causality
4-80. Individual subjectivity builds global collaboration
4-81. Individual subjectivity leads historical evolution
4-82. Individuality integrates subject of love and object of happiness
4-83. The "principle of integration of love" and the "principle of domination of ONSHU"
4-84. The earth star is the planet of legalized domination structure
4-85. The dominating structure of the brain is the center of physical domination
4-86. The physical dominating structure is the root of all evil in the "rule of reincarnation"
4-87. The dominating structure on the earth star is the unique structure of the universe
4-88. Manifestation of "SHINSEI integration consciousness" world by PARAREVO
4-89. The true view of life and death based on the "rule of the attainment of spiritual being during life"
4-90. The 21st century is the watershed in human history
4-91. How do we resolve discrimination in the world?
4-92. How do we resolve the gap between rich and poor?

4-93. How do we resolve the disparity in civilization?
4-94. How do we resolve the religious conflicts?
4-95. Free from the boundaries between race and nations
4-96. Equation for releasing core of ONSHU
4-97. Transition to female supremacy from male supremacy
4-98. The way for solving problems on the earth
4-99. Challenge "the era of termination" in religions
4-100. The theory of PARAREVO is the thought of remorse
4-101. Homo-cosmology and "Regeneration of SHINSEI and soul"

For more information please contact us :
Self-Healing Study and Practice Group
(info@selfhealing.co.in)

www.ingramcontent.com/pod-product-compliance
Lightning Source LLC
Chambersburg PA
CBHW070741160426
43192CB00009B/1529